THE FLAMES SHALL NOT CONSUME YOU

Mary Ellen Ton

David C. Cook Publishing Co.

ELGIN, ILLINOIS—WESTON, ONTARIO

MARY ELLEN TON is coordinator of the Wishard Hospital
Burn Unit in Indianapolis, Indiana. She is the wife of the
Reverend Eugene Ton, executive minister of the Indianapo-
lis Baptist Association.

Mary Ellen has written one other book, *For the Love of My
Daughter*, and numerous articles for *Today's Christian
Woman*, *The Baptist Leader*, and *Guideposts*. Mary Ellen
and her husband have three sons—Jack, Jeffrey, and Joel—
and a daughter, Jill.

Published by David C. Cook Publishing Co., Elgin, IL 60120. Cover design and illustration by
Britt Taylor Collins.

Printed in the United States of America.
ISBN: 0-89191-556-7
LC: 81-71993

To each person who, for the love of me,
came into my fiery furnace,
bringing life in their hands.
This one's for you.

CONTENTS

Acknowledgments

Just a few days ago I sat in a small office outside Wishard Memorial Hospital's burn unit talking to one of the nurses.

"Sometimes I look at our patients and wonder if we have really done them any favor by saving their lives," she said. "I wonder if I would want to face the rest of my life disfigured, perhaps without hands or feet."

I could not answer her immediately. For a few minutes I reflected on how I had felt about the doctors and nurses who had saved my life after my journey through fire. At one point I was not at all certain they had done me a kindness. But after considering her comment, I replied, "What I see you doing is offering a gift—the gift of a second chance at life. What a patient does with the gift is up to them. But without the gift, there would be no choice."

These are just a few of the persons who brought that gift to me: David J. Smith, Jr., M.D.; Bernard Swartz, M.D.; Kent Yamaguchi, M.D.; Jane Caldwell-Gwin, R.N., A.H.N.; Ernest Klein, R.N., A.H.N.; Carolyn Milan, R.N., A.H.N.; Mary Stegman, R.N., A.H.N.; Sharon Ehrsam, R.N.; Lisa Hobson, R.N.; Brenda Keeley, R.N.; Lavada Stockard, R.N.; Marinel Watness, R.N.; Edie York, R.N.; Ed Bryan, L.P.N.; Gerry Easter, L.P.N.; Rita Harmon, L.P.N.; Ruth Leavell, L.P.N.; Shirley McMann, L.P.N.; Becky Nail,

L.P.N.; India Ryhal, L.P.N.; Lonnie Wissel, L.P.N.; Marie Ambuehl, N.A.; Sherry Hall, R.P.T.; Heidi Hermann, O.T.R.; Juli Howell, R.P.T.; Bill Gaither, P.T. assistant; Charlene Perry Clark, W.S.; Carol Shearer, W.S.; José Esquibel, Zenaita Avila, Linda Harvey, housekeepers; Marti Vores, social worker; Father Joseph M. Barry, O.M.I., chaplain; Morgan Mansfield, paramedic; Linda Bancroft, paramedic; Jim Glad, E.M.T.; Kevin Wilmouth, E.M.T.; Michael Rosinski, E.M.T.; Barry Green, paramedic; Sue Rhee, dietician.

My family brought another gift—the gift of a "why." Friedrich Wilhelm Nietzsche wrote: "He who has a why to live can bear with almost any how." My "why to live" was given to me by my husband, Gene, and my children: Jack; Jill, her husband, Bill McGregor, and son, Jeffrey; Jeffrey, his wife, Vicki, and son, Jeremy; and Joel and his wife, Janet.

There were others: the rest of my family, countless friends, and even persons I have never met, who held out to me a special gift of hope: that, not only would I live, but that I would live life abundantly.

The writing of this book brought its own gift as I was challenged to live the ending of my own story—an ending that would proclaim the power within the Christian community to call forth life from the midst of deathlike experiences. Janet Hoover Thoma, my editor, Mary Stegman, R.N., A.H.N., who read my manuscript for medical accuracy, and Claribel Carson, who typed and retyped countless pages, enabled me in the writing process.

In a very real sense, each of these persons is one of the authors of this book.

1

Ladybug, Ladybug, Fly Away Home

January 4, 1980. A date as indelibly engraved on my mind as the day of my birth. It began like so many other days. The alarm went off at 5:45 A.M. I dragged my body to the shower to the music of WXTZ—the "old people's radio station," my rock fan sons called it.

By the time I had my makeup on and was blow drying my hair, I was wide awake and looked back at my reflection with satisfaction. I felt no conceit in admitting that I liked the way I looked. After all, I was God's handiwork.

Gene and I breakfasted on coffee and stollen left over from New Year's, grabbed our coats, and went out into the garage. Just before we each crawled into our own car, we shared the perfunctory kiss of the twenty-eight-year married and said, "Bye. See you tonight."

How casually said and how easily assumed those words were!

How were we to know our "tonight" would not come that day? Before lunch our tonights and tomorrows would all be irrevocably changed.

Only twenty minutes later, I unlocked the office door and punched the time clock. Since the Edna Martin Christian Center in Indianapolis, Indiana, had moved its administrative offices to the Woodruff Place Baptist Church, I had enjoyed having windows in my section. Even though these were frosted glass, the sunshine brightened my days. I pushed open the window for fresh air, and then closed it again just before I got out my books. There were a few big, lazy snowflakes falling like feathers past my second floor observation site.

The first of any month is a busy time for a bookkeeper. The first of the new year is doubly so. That is why I was working on this Friday, which was to have been my day off. In addition to balancing out for December, there were also claims to prepare for filing. Title XX, CETA, School Lunch, WIN, all were essential to the center in its hand-to-mouth existence. The sooner they were in, the sooner our coffers would be filled to meet the next payroll.

The center had greatly expanded since it was begun by Dr. Edna Martin, a most lovely and gracious black woman. Dr. Edna didn't wait for ERA or Women's Lib to go out and do her thing. Years before those movements were even envisioned, she began a ministry to economically deprived blacks on the east side of Indianapolis. Her "car ran on faith," as the old saying goes, and she lived to see the work of her hands move from the condemned, rat-infested building where it had all begun to a brand-new facility. Now the center maintained two satellite programs, one of which was housed in the Woodruff Place Baptist Church.

As the minutes turned into hours, I found myself becoming even more deeply engrossed. Having worked on two jobs where interruptions were ordinary and confusion reigned, I had learned to block out everything around me. I only vaguely took notice when LaVern Young, the administrator's assistant, stuck her head in my door to tell me she and Frank Shirly, the program associate at Woodruff Place, were going to pick up supplies and then get some lunch. I turned down an invitation to join them, explaining I would just finish the report I was working on and go home to get ready for our weekend guests.

Returning to my columns of figures, the rhythmic clicking of my calculator blocked out everything else. Then rustlinglike noises came from someplace down the hall, trying to coax me away from my work. I tried even harder to concentrate, but an acrid odor burned my nose. I could even taste it in my mouth. I casually wondered what was being fixed in the building now.

Just recently the church had converted the furnace from oil to gas. Workers with welding torches had made our noses aware of their presence. And a few weeks ago a ballast had burned out in a fluorescent light fixture, causing so much alarm with the smoke and smell that we had called the fire department.

I continued to punch the little numbers onto a tape while the odor grew even stronger, now burning my throat. I was irritated by this further distraction that challenged my power of concentration.

Suddenly there was a loud noise, like doors being forced open to bang against a wall. It sounded as if it came from right outside my door. The room that houses LaVern's office and mine was divided down the middle by a partition. My office was toward the outside wall and a doorway in the partition led to hers. Her office was the only one that opened directly into the hallway. From my desk against the partition, I could see neither LaVern's office nor the hall.

Uneasy, I got up and moved around to where I could look through the adjoining office into the hall. I was stunned by the sight that assaulted my eyes. It looked as though a black curtain had been dropped over the open doorway—a curtain that was billowing in a wind. It was smoke—thick, black, and swirling.

I moved back to my desk and picked up the phone. What was the number to call in an emergency? The telephone directory was on the bookcase behind me. But I knew there wasn't time. In my mind, I saw the hall and the metal folding gate that closed it off from the rest of the building just to the left of our office door. The gate had been erected to keep the children involved in our program from wandering around in the rest of the church building.

And it was kept locked. Where was the key? On my desk? In my purse? Again I had the instinctive feeling there was no time. No time to call the fire department. No time to unlock a gate. No time to run down the hall, down the stairs, and out of this place. I was trapped!

The noises I had assumed to be other persons at work were actually the cracklings of a fire working its way towards me. To this day, when I sit near the fireplace in my home listening to the flames sputter and sizzle, I cannot fathom why I did not immediately recognize those sounds drifting down the hallway.

I had the incredulous feeling I was watching a television show. This couldn't be happening to me. But it was. I knew I had to get help. The window. I would call out the window. I turned the handle and pushed the window open for the second time that day. With a great whooshing sound and a roar like a dry Christmas tree burning, the heat and the smoke leaped to the open window and began their destruction of me.

For a brief instant, I thought someone had come to rescue me. The impact of the intense heat on my body made me think a huge and powerfully strong person had lunged at my back, pounding his weight against me, slamming me with arms that encircled me and pushed me against the window. My arms shot upwards as if to signal my surrender as every muscle and sinew tightened to ward off this assault. A giant convulsion shook my body as I turned from person to pain.

There was no pulling away from the grip fastened on me as I might have done from contact with a hot burner on the stove. I could not quickly drop the offender, like a hot spoon handle. There was no escape. My enemy was merciless as it ate away at my flesh, destroying forever the image I had known.

A woman's voice was screaming: "Help, help, somebody help me." It was my voice. The alley, usually filled during lunch hour with kids from Arsenal Tech High School across the street was empty; the school was still closed for the holidays. Only the broken asphalt of the alley and the bricks in the wall of the next building heard my screams.

Quickly I slammed the window shut. I let my body sink to the floor, leaning on the wall under the window. And then I prayed. No pretty words. No nice sounding phrases. But the only words I had: "Oh, God . . . Oh, my God . . . God." Some people use God's name in that way as a curse. For me, at that moment, it was a committal. It was as if I had said, "It is finished."

How I climbed out the window, I do not know. I have no recollection of opening the window again. The next thing I remember I was hanging onto the windowsill with my fingers, my body suspended above the alley to East Michigan Street. Cars sped by below. Again I screamed: "Help, help, oh, please, help me."

The heat and smoke pursued me out the window, clutching me in their searing arms as I tried to escape the holocaust inside. With the flames drawing rapidly closer, the superheated gases devoured the skin on my hands. I desperately tried to maintain my hold on the windowsill as the burning heat feasted on pieces of the face that had smiled back at me from the bathroom mirror just a few hours earlier.

A car seemed to slow down. Had someone seen me? But the car scarcely stopped and then was gone. I loosened my fingers and dropped two stories to the frozen ground below.

I had often wondered what someone who committed suicide by jumping to their death felt as their body hit the ground. I felt nothing on impact—absolutely nothing. I just knew I was down and I was still alive. I had landed on an ole coal-chute cover, denting the steel. I slid off my four-foot-high landing pad and groped my way down the alley toward the street, the cars, the people—still calling out for help.

A sound from behind me caused me to turn around. A man was coming down the alley toward me. On any other occasion I probably would have thought of him as a potential enemy. Now he was a savior. I sunk to the ground, which was still covered with some remnants of the last snow, giving up my fight for life and putting my body into the hands of strangers. The nerve endings in my skin had been totally destroyed, and I could no longer feel the pain of the second- and third-degree burns that covered over half my body.

"The fire department has been called and an ambulance is on the way," the stranger told me. He *had* seen me hanging onto the ledge. His car had slowed down and started up again to go around the corner, where he had called for the help that was needed.

"Please," I asked him, "please, call my husband. Tell him I love him."

People began to gather there in the mud and debris of the alley. "Please," I asked him again, "please tell my husband I love him."

Then came the lonely sound of a siren wailing. The same sound that had always scared me a little, causing me to wonder where my family was at that moment. Now that wail brought assurance. Help was on the way.

The ambulance parked near me in the alley. A paramedic began to cut the burned clothes off my body. I reiterated the same message: "Call my husband. Please. Tell him I love him." To me that was most important.

"What is his number?" a voice asked.

"I don't know. I don't know. Reverend Eugene Ton. *T-O-N*," I spelled, "Indianapolis—Baptist—Association." I enunciated the words carefully, pausing between each one. To some people it seemed like such an odd place to work, not like Eli Lilly or Allison's. They must understand. They must reach him. I needed to get my message to him and, besides, he would know what to do. "Please, call him. Tell him I love him."

Funny! When everything else is stripped away, all that really matters is love.

Hands continued to move over me, taking the disinte-grated synthetic materials away from the burned flesh. Someone in the crowd was hysterically crying, "Help this woman. Please help this woman." There were children standing nearby. Why didn't someone think to take them away? Why not protect them from the ugliness of life for a little while longer?

I started again to ask someone to call Gene and was assured his office had been reached. Another voice asked, "Was she wearing gloves?"

Why would they ask that, I wondered. I opened my eyes and looked down my arm to my hand. There, hanging from my fingertips, was something that certainly did look like a rubber glove. It was my own skin.

Arms started to lift me, and a terrible pain shot through my back. "My back. Oh, my back," I cried out. The arms lifted me into the ambulance while a voice crackled on the radio. Someone kept asking my name. *Why do they keep asking me that? I already told them,* I thought. But I dutifully responded again, "Mary Ellen Ton."

The person who was working over me started to tell the voice on the radio what my injuries were in their own secret code. The siren began to wail out the misery of its passen-ger. I heard someone say, "Estimated time of arrival—fifteen minutes." It sounded like a line from a television show.

When I arrived at the hospital, fluid resuscitation was begun immediately. The destruction of my skin would cause a massive shift of my body's fluids. Once the IV was in place and my stability was determined, I was placed in the hydrotherapy tank to clean the burns, removing charred clothing and dead skin. This stainless steel tank, sometimes referred to as a Hubbard tank, looks like a giant, ginger-bread-man cookie cutter.

Life became a series of slow-motion film clips. I felt as if I was floating in a tank of water, my arms and legs flailing to keep myself from sinking, when actually I was lying quite securely on a plinth or plastic stretcher. I was in shock and had already been given some drugs, which distorted the shapes of persons and things surrounding me.

People were talking to each other, doing things to me, asking questions. "What is your name? How old are you? Are you allergic to any drugs?"

"Have you ever had heart trouble? High blood pressure? Diabetes? Hepatitis? Do you smoke? Drink? Are you taking any drugs?"

And back to the beginning, "Can you tell me your name?" People. Taking off my rings . . . my necklace . . . my earrings.

I was scarcely aware of those who tended me that first day. The team of doctors was only a large group of faceless people who swept in and out of my room like a wave. Except for Dr. Yamaguchi, who is Japanese. I was aware he was Oriental and that he spoke softly and touched gently. To my befuddled mind he was my niece Barbara's husband, who is Chinese and a doctor of pathology.

"Please," I asked the nurses, "tell my husband I love him." Somewhere in the room I could see a red light. Did they drive the ambulance right up to the tank? In reality the light was a heat lamp to help maintain my body's normal temperature. With a major portion of my skin destroyed, I had lost my insulation.

At last a nurse said, "Your husband is here. Gene is here."

Oh, good news. Now everything would be all right. *Where is he?* "Where is he?"

"You'll see him in a little while when you are ready to go to your room."

Hands seemed to reach for me from every direction as the long, arduous task of debridement was begun. To a newly admitted burn victim like myself, this nice-sounding medical term meant that my burned skin would be removed bit by bit by scrubbing with surgical sponges with plastic bristles on one side and cutting with scalpels or scissors until each area of my body's surface was clean.

Debridement is an ugly job. The water was soon colored with my blood. Pieces of my removed skin floated on its surface. Although it was almost two weeks before I was taken to the tank again, the memory of that first night remained firmly entrenched in my mind, haunting me every day of my stay in the burn unit.

"Are you all right, Mrs. Ton? Mary Ellen, open your eyes. Just open your eyes so I'll know you're all right."

I did not remember hearing that nurse's voice before. The shift had changed since my admittance. I opened my eyes, but what I saw was dark and confusing, so I shut them again.

I was in a bed now. I could not move, but it was all right. I didn't even want to. A soft, frightened sounding voice called, "Honey?"

For that voice I would open my eyes.

Gene bent low over me and I looked at his face. It was the most beautiful face I had ever seen. "I got your message." His voice choked over the words.

2

The Answer, My Friend, Is Blowin' in the Wind . . .

Gene had arrived at Wishard Hospital four hours earlier. His secretary had located him at the Indianapolis Athletic Club, where he had gone for lunch. Two thoughts were uppermost in his mind when he strode through the emergency entrance: first, that I was already dead and no one had wanted to tell him; second, that he wanted to get me out of County Hospital. Like most other county hospitals, Wishard had an unfavorable reputation in Indianapolis. But Gene did not know how fortunate I was to have been taken directly to one of only two specialized burn units within the state of Indiana.

When the nurse suggested, "I will take you to the Quiet Room," in a subdued voice, Gene's worst fear had been confirmed. Every minister knew the Quiet Room had just one purpose: to provide a secluded place for a doctor or chaplain to inform family members of the impending death—or death—of a loved one.

Gene tried to get more details of what had happened from the nurse. He learned that I had been trapped in the fire because the iron gate in the hallway had been locked, and there were no exits out of my office.

"That _ _ _ _ gate!" Gene exploded, "That _ _ _ _ gate!" He slammed his fist into the wall. There was so much emotion broiling in him: fear, frustration, helplessness, and rage that had no object. In those moments the gate became the object. It became the "guilty one."

Two months before I had sat at my desk and watched that gate as it had been installed across the hallway, never realizing that it was blocking an escape route. Neither I nor anyone else at Woodruff Place Baptist Church had realized that the church was violating an ordinance of the fire code by closing off an exit with a metal folding gate. Nor did the building contain a simple smoke detector, costing less than $20.00, which would have warned me so I would have had time to make it to the front door. Ironically, I had been as relieved as anyone when a health department representative or a fire inspector went easy on our facilities.

It was later discovered that the fire was started by a defective cord on a small hot pot, which had been left plugged into a wall socket. The fire that changed my life should never have happened!

For the next several hours, Gene, with our son Jeff and his wife, Vicki, played the "waiting game"—wondering, thinking, going over and over the little they knew, and making guesses about what they didn't. The agony of those who wait is often untold in the unfolding drama of a life-and-death struggle. Some hide their thoughts in the secret recesses of their own hearts, unable to let them out; others find a release in vocalizing them.

After a long time, a nurse came into the room. Gene jumped up and almost pounced on her.

"Mary Ellen's alive," she assured them. "She is coherent and wants me to tell you she loves you," she said, looking at Gene. "The doctor will be out to talk to you as soon as we have finished cleaning her up. Just as soon as she is in her room, you can see her." With that short summary, the nurse returned to the burn unit.

She had not indicated how serious things were, but she was so warm and so confident, Gene began to feel a little more secure. "It sounds as if she's in good hands," he said as much to reassure himself as Jeff and Vicki.

With the nurse's words, "She wants me to tell you she

loves you," ringing in his ears, Gene turned to the wall, beating on it with the palms of his hands. "She can't die. She can't die. . . . Not now. She doesn't know how much I love her."

Jeff and Vicki knew how desperately important those words were to both Gene and me. We had been traveling some pretty rocky ground. Our marriage had been shaken and bounced and even suffered badly skinned knees. They were not uncommon problems—until they became our own and not someone else's: job changes, a move from Evansville to Indianapolis, and a change of roles as Gene went from pastor to executive (which precipitated a new search for identity and his own mid-life crisis) and I went from pastor's wife to "nothing." Then there had been a six-month separation while our youngest son, Joe, finished high school in Evansville. In trying to find our way through this maze, Gene's counseling experience didn't help us. We found ourselves making the same mistakes others before us had made. Turning everywhere for answers except to each other, it was inevitable that the big question should loom up: "Did we really still love each other?"

News of the fire spread as quickly around Indianapolis that afternoon as the flames had through the office. Minister friends began arriving at the small room outside the burn unit. The frightened family waiting there was amazed at this outpouring of love and caring. To my son Jeff it was almost unbelievable; it had all seemed so phony to him before. Now he realized this caring was what his father had done many times. As a child and teenager, Jeff had resented the intrusion into our family life. The phone would ring and, no matter what was going on, his dad would take off.

Now, in our family's time of need, clergy friends had come to run errands, take care of business left hanging at Gene's office, pick up Granny Ton at nearby Lebanon, Indiana, and take her to the house to take care of the countless phone calls. In such a way a web of love was fashioned around us, each person offering the varicolored threads of their thoughtfulness.

Finally, at about 5:15 P.M., approximately four hours after Gene had arrived at the hospital, a nurse came to tell him that Dr. Yamaguchi was ready to talk to him.

Jeff, Vicki, and Gene followed her into a plain, simple office. They wanted to know the truth about my condition, but, now that the time had come, they were afraid to be told.

Fifty-five percent of my body surface was burned, Dr. Yamaguchi explained. "Over a third of these burns are third degree, the most severe. Her arms, hands, scalp, back, neck, shoulders, and the sides of her trunk were burned. Most of the severe burns are above the waist, with some on the left leg. Her hands were injured severely."

"What about her face?" It was my daughter-in-law, Vicki, who thought to ask.

"Her face was burned, too, although the full extent will not be known for days," he said.

"Was there any other injury?" Once again Vicki thought of the question.

"Yes, her back. It is possible there has been a fractured vertebra. And," Dr. Yamaguchi continued, "there has been lung damage. That is the immediate danger."

Dr. Yamaguchi said something more about black specks coming up in the mucus, but the minds of the listeners were whirring with information they had no experience to understand. Their incredulity at what had happened showed in their faces.

"A nurse will come get you in a few minutes to take you to see her," the doctor went on. He spoke in hopeful, confident terms as he told them the staff would keep a close watch during the next critical forty-eight hours, taking appropriate steps as needed.

Gene and the kids returned to their temporary home, the family waiting room, fearful, but strangely relieved now that they knew exactly what had happened. During the next hour they talked about everything Dr. Yamaguchi had told them, rehearsing every detail of the new information, until a nurse opened the door and walked in.

Warning they could only visit for ten minutes each hour, she proceeded to give explicit instructions about entering the burn unit. Infection was a serious threat to a burn victim, she told them, so stiff, wrinkled yellow gowns would be put on over their street clothes. They were told to carefully wash their hands and to wear a face mask if they had any cold symptoms. Later Gene was instructed to wear plastic gloves when he performed any service for me, such as applying ointment to my lips.

Hands washed, dressed in the gowns, with Jeff wearing a mask, Gene and Jeff followed the nurse to the double doors, which shut the burn unit off from the rest of the hospital. Gene stopped. "I'm scared!"

Jeff put his hand on his father's shoulder, and together they walked through the doors into another hall. Halfway down, the nurse who was leading them turned into a room.

Nothing could have prepared them for what they were looking at once they entered my room. I was in the midst of tubes and lights and graphs, wrapped in gauze like a mummy. Swelling had already taken away my familiar facial characteristics. "See you tonight," I had said. Now almost to the minute when Gene would have walked through the kitchen door to find me fixing dinner, he saw a figure his mind refused to recognize as me until I began to speak in answer to his soft, questioning, "Honey?"

"I was just sitting at my desk working," I began to talk, the words rapidly flowing out, rehearsing what had happened, almost like one who witnessed something terrible but was not really a part of it. Then, "I'm so sorry. I'm so sorry to cause you all this trouble."

"Don't . . . don't say that. If anyone's to blame, it's me. I was the one who suggested you go to work there in the first place."

"I know, but . . . the whole last year . . . it's been so awful for you. I made it awful. I . . . ."

"Sh-h-h-h-h, it doesn't matter," Gene interrupted, and

then tried to turn our thoughts in another direction by asking, "Are you hurting? Is the pain very bad for you?"

We didn't speak of the past year again for almost two months. But it was there in the room as we both tried to assure the other of our love and begged forgiveness with our eyes. We both wondered if we had lost a race with time.

The ten minutes passed too quickly, and Gene was not ready to leave me. He stepped into the hall, where Jeff was waiting, and they returned to the family room. Although they felt better now, all the tubes, monitors, and hovering nurses told them not to set their hopes too high.

Sitting on a couch, Vicki's arm around him, Jeff rattled on and on: "Mom doesn't look human. It sounds terrible to say, I know, but she reminds me of 'The Thing,' from that cartoon, 'The Fantastic Four.' Her lips looked like two hot dogs. . . .

"Vicki, I couldn't take it. I had to leave. I fought it. I bit my lip to stop it from quivering. Mom's in there in all that pain, and I couldn't stay in the room with her . . . . I think she's going to die."

Up until then, Jeff had held onto an inner feeling that everything would be all right. God would keep me from dying. Growing up in a minister's home, he had seldom questioned his faith's teachings. Our God is a God of love. He cares about us. Don't worry about food, he will feed you. Don't worry about clothes, he will clothe you. Don't worry about fire, he will . . . let you burn?

"Why, Vicki? Why would God allow this to happen to someone like mom? What did she ever do to deserve this? She loved God. Why did he turn his back on her? Is the whole God bit a bunch of bull? I don't understand. . . . I just don't understand."

In another corner of the room, Gene sat listening. He had no ready answers to offer—only more and even deeper questions.

The time passed slowly for Gene, Jeff, and Vicki as they waited out each hour on the clock for the brief ten-minute interval in my room. The tension was relieved each time the door opened, and another family member joined their fearful vigil.

Joe, my youngest son, and Janet, his fiancee, arrived first. At 9:00 P.M., almost eight hours after the fire, my daughter, Jill, her husband, Bill, and Jack, my oldest son, entered the small waiting room, completing the family circle. There was great comfort in everyone's being there. The trip from Evansville had seemed interminably long as each one silently wondered if I would be alive when they reached the hospital.

As the hands of the clock dictated someone's release from that room into mine, it was determined Jill should be next to visit me. But when she stepped into my room, the machines and tubes looked awesome. What bothered her most was that she couldn't recognize the person lying on the bed as her mother.

I rambled on about sheets in the linen closet at home and where she would find blankets and pillows, while Jill searched every inch of the bed for something familiar. All she recognized in that entire room were my shoes under a table across from the bed. It almost made her ill to see them because she knew I had been wearing them when it happened.

And then her eyes fell on my fingertips. They were black. Black! Jill couldn't imagine how they had gotten so black. She didn't want to. She tried to shut the sight from her mind but it didn't go away . . . not for a long time.

They were all in shock that night, so exhausted, but not ready to give in to sleep. The guys tried to sack out on the floor, but, for the most part, it was useless. They each feared the worst, but wouldn't say it. Jill paced the halls with Gene, and they talked about guilt and the horrible thing that had happened.

Jill wrestled with her conscience all through the night. *Shouldn't I be praying for her life? But, first of all, would it do any good? What was God doing at 12:00 that day? And,* besides, should I pray for her life if she has to live through unbearable pain, horrible scarring, and possibly never use her hands again? Should I wish that on my mother? She wouldn't want it.

But how can I bear to lose her?

3

Suddenly I'm Not Half
The Girl I Used to Be

Everything is strange, I thought. Strange to be lying here all wrapped up. Strange the shrill *beep, beep, beep* of the monitors. Sounds like a microwave oven. And then strange voices, speaking in secret code language: CBC (complete blood count), BUN (blood urea nitrogen), CRIT (hemoglobin hematocrit), IV (intravenous).

It was my turn to ask those who were in the room with me, "What is your name?"

Strange names came back from someplace in the room: "Sharon . . . Mary . . . Carolyn . . . Marinel . . . Ernie . . ."

Strange the look on Gene's face and Jeff's. They looked so afraid, so worn. Strange to be floating about the room like this. Strange the things it seemed so important to tell Gene. I felt I must tell him about that room: the smoke and the burning heat, hanging from the second-floor window, calling for help.

I tried to tell him how it was. But it was so difficult to talk. The bandages were wrapped too tightly around my throat. When it was Gene's turn to visit again, I tried to tell him why it was so hard to talk. "I think they bandaged my neck too tight."

It was getting increasingly uncomfortable, as though a scarf had been tied around my neck and was slowly being drawn tighter and tighter. No one seemed to be concerned.

28

At least no one came to loosen the Kerlix bandage. I couldn't see Gene very well, either. If he stood erect beside my bed, he was out of my view. But if he bent over right in front of me, I could make him out.

More than anything else, it was the faces of my kids and Gene that conveyed the seriousness of what had happened. The silent message in their eyes betrayed the fear in their hearts and told me my unseen roommate was death.

I was not afraid of dying. I was more concerned that my vision was growing more and more limited and the tightness around my neck was making it difficult to breathe.

The extreme facial swelling at last closed my eyes completely. My world was black, filled with unidentifiable sounds and voices. The only familiar thing left was the subdued, frightened words from those who stood watch through the long night: "I love you, mom." "I love you, honey." "I love you." "I love you."

About one o'clock in the morning, I again tried to tell someone about the distress the tight bandages were causing. "The bandages are too tight around my neck." I barely croaked out the words to a nurse who always seemed to be sitting at the foot of my bed.

There was a flurry of excitement. From the family room, Gene heard someone running down the hall. He watched the anesthesiologist turn into my room. When I had first complained of the tightness, Dr. Yamaguchi told him my throat was swelling. The nurses had been well aware of my discomfort and were keeping a close watch. With unexpected suddenness, my throat swelled shut, closing off my airway. I felt the pushing and pressure as the naso-trachaeo tube was quickly and expertly inserted. Then just as I began to "crow," a term used by the nurses for the sound emitted by a suffocating patient, I felt the rush of cool oxygen filling my lungs.

The respirator breathed for me. It pushed the life-sustaining oxygen into my lungs and I exhaled it. If I became too tired, or if I deliberately stopped breathing—wishing to just quietly slip away—the machine set off its tattletale *beep, beep, beep.* Instantly from the end of my bed came a loud voice commanding, "Breathe, Mary Ellen. Take a breath. Breathe." There seemed always to be a nurse someplace in my room.

Later I would learn one of them had sat on a high stool beside the raised bedside table my charts were on, constantly observing my struggle for life. It was as though they would not *let* me die, their voices ordering me to take the next breath of life. And when the strange birdlike *beep* stopped as my breathing was regulated, the voice crooned, "That's good! You're doing fine. Just keep it up."

That machine was holding out life to me while my lungs healed, but it also deprived me of an important part of living. As long as I was intubated, I could not talk. There was so much I needed to tell my family. But I could not speak the words, and I could not see their faces. For a brief period of time, I entered the strange world of the blind and the mute. It is a dark and frighteningly lonely world.

Somehow I must talk to them! On Saturday, the day after the accident, I found I could raise my right arm with great difficulty to wave at them. I was bombarded with questions I had no way to answer: "What is it? Do you need something? What's the matter?"

I began to draw letters in the air, even though I couldn't see my hands forming the shapes. Slowly, awkwardly, painfully, I sketched the letter *A* over and over. As different members of the family visited, I tried again. Each one tried to guess at what I was trying to communicate. Finally someone said, "*A.* Is it an *A*?"

I nodded my head as best I could and drew a *B*.

"*B*," they responded, and then, "*C*."

Now I could talk to them. I would not be closed off in my separate corner of the world. Patiently, they recited the alphabet as I nodded at the letter that was right.

Jill rapidly became adept at alphabetizing with me. Her quick mind reasoned out the use of vowels and their relation to consonants, which expedited the whole procedure. I could get my messages across to her accurately and quickly. It was Jill I must give my most important words to.

Even though I couldn't see her, I could feel her beside me, her tummy, which was large in the eighth month of pregnancy, brushing the sheets of my bed. My only daughter. This was her first child. I knew she was an emotionally fragile person, inheriting this quality, I supposed, from her mother. I was worried about her as the shaky, choked-up tone of her voice spoke of her tremendous anxiety. Jill and I had traveled a long, rough, many detoured road together. (That story is told in my first book, *For the Love of My Daughter*.[1]) Perhaps because we knew both the best and worst about each other, we had drawn closer and closer together in the past several years. One day she had said to me, "Mother, I think you are my best friend."

Jill had stood beside me through Gene's and my struggle to reestablish our relationship. Reaching out. Caring. Trying to understand. Giving encouragement as she repeatedly affirmed, "Mom, I *know* dad loves you. I believe that." Until I told her, "Jill, you are so much more than a daughter to me, you are my friend."

Now I knew she would understand and accept my words. So I began. I raised my hand to indicate I had something I wanted to say.

"A, E, I," she listed the vowels, and I nodded at *I*.

"Is there more to the word?"

I shook my head. "You want to say, 'you'?" she queried.

I nodded and we went on. *I . . . AM . . . NOT . . . AFRAID . . . TO . . . DIE.*

"Oh, mom," Jill cried.

I raised my hand.

"There's more?" she asked softly.

Again I nodded. *I . . . KNOW . . . GOD.*

"I know you do. I know you do."

I was tired from the strain, but there was one more thing

I wanted to say to her husband, Bill. He had been beside Jill the entire time. I had felt his presence rather than known it, because after a quiet, "Hi, Mary Ellen," he had been silent.

Jill and I wiped the board clean and started the whole process over until I had spelled, *I . . . LOVE . . . YOU*, and pointed my hand at Bill.

Bill had entered Jill's life at its lowest ebb. Her first marriage had ended after only a year and a half. It had been a disaster from the beginning, with both of the young people struggling their way through a maze of conflicting expectations for themselves and each other. The sense of failure was a heavy load, added to an already overstuffed bag of guilt from the past of a teenager who had struggled with rebellion and her own sense of identity.

As in the proverbial fairy tale, Bill, the handsome prince, had kissed my Jill, and turned her into the beautiful princess she was always intended to be. Now I had let him know how much I appreciated his love for her. My words *I love you* had communicated my thanks.

There were other messages I gave my visitors. Some expressed my inner concerns and fears, and some were as silly as bemoaning the new bra I had just bought for ten dollars, which I knew was now only a burned fragment. But to each one—Jack, my firstborn; Jeff, and his wife, Vicki; Joe, my "baby," and Janet, then his fiancee, and especially to Gene—I spelled: "I love you." They were each so special to me, as was my first grandson, Jeff's baby, Jeremy. Why had I waited until there was so little time and no words to tell them how much they meant to me?

Without any warning, my world had gone. Disappeared. Yesterday I had no idea that this morning I would be wearing Kerlix and Kling bandages, with Silvadene ointment as my body lotion and the stench of burnt flesh replacing my Moonwind cologne. Gold earrings were no longer important; my earlobes were gone. New vests, treasured leather purses, even records and financial reports, faded into insignificance. Suddenly, I knew I wasn't the same

Mary Ellen. That person had vanished and in her place . . .

I would not think about that now. I couldn't. I was in the drug-induced euphoria where time has no beginning and no end, and places and things are only a part of the fantasy. There was only one reality: my family. Every time I opened my eyes, one or two of them hovered nearby. When I wanted to stay in Morphine Land, drifting about in my room or leaving it for places where there was cool, green grass to lie down in, their voices called me back: "Mary? . . . Mary? . . . Honey?"

"Hang on, mom. I love you. We need you."

"Fight, honey, fight. Don't give up on us. I love you. It should be me there, not you."

Even when I imagined I was a child and had crawled up onto God's lap to be gently rocked, their love would not let me go.

Then, on my first Sunday morning in Wishard's burn unit, an incredible thing began to happen. In Baptist churches in Indianapolis, and stretching out into other parts of Indiana, Wisconsin, Pennsylvania, and places we didn't even know about, the news of my personal disaster spread. Persons began to pray. Not one or two. Not fifty or sixty. But whole congregations, hundreds and hundreds of people interceding for me.

And in a small, nondescript hospital room, which was part of the huge Indiana University Medical School complex, eight persons stood around my bed. Jack, Jill and Bill, Jeff and Vicki, Joe and Janet, and Gene joined hands around my bed and passed our family cup from one to another.

We had adopted as our own the rich history of the cup running through the pages of the Old and New Testaments.[2] In the Psalms, the cup symbolizes the happiness and the bitterness of man's life. Jesus spoke of the cup of impending suffering. For Christians, the cup has become most significant in the service of Holy Communion. Our family cup of blessing had been passed in celebration of birthdays, engagements, weddings, births, and many special holidays. It was our custom to give "unseen" gifts: ones that could not be bought, but could only be given as someone unwrapped his heart. As we had passed the cup, we had offered our gifts of love or blessing to the person whose special occasion was being commemorated.

On January 6, 1980, this family cup was shared around my hospital bed. The day before, the family had discussed their plans for Sunday, and all agreed that their feelings were too raw to go to church. Yet, the need to give expression to their faith was real and vital.

I could not see them as they came quietly into my room to circle my bed. Unseen, too, were the gifts offered as each person held the cup in their hands, and tried somehow to express the anguish and hope of their hearts. Each sounded uncertain as to whether they had gathered to celebrate my life or mourn my death.

Some had words to clothe their thoughts; some didn't. Their feelings went nakedly and unashamedly to God. Just as I had so often done on other occasions, Jeff chose to write his thoughts. The poem he shared expressed everyone's feelings of thankfulness that there were windows in my office, which had become my escape from the fire.

It's a window into sunshine,
A window into light.
It's a window to help plants grow;
It's a window to let love flow.

Even now the flames leap.
Even now the smoke stinks.
Even now my skin burns.
God, why did I even try?

My senses are closing in on me.
I can't talk; I can't see.
Every nerve screams to die.
My God, I can't even cry.

The cup was passed by nine,
Touching every lip, but mine.
It was then it came to me,
All that it meant to be.

It was a window into sunshine,
A window into light.
It was a window to let love flow.
But, little did I know,
It was a window into life.

Tears and laughter had been a part of our cup celebrations in the past. In what was the heaviest moment in any of
our lives, Jack brought smiles through the tears as he teased,
"Mom, this was one heck of a way to get us all together."

I, who had always been the nurturer, the giver, now
became the receiver. As the IV pumped life-sustaining fluids
into my body, my family joined hands around my bed to
infuse my spirit with life-giving love. I was not left out of the
circle because of my burned hands. Two persons' fingertips
reached out to rest gently on my right foot.

4

Pain, Pain, Go Away
Come Again Some Other Day

Live. Die. Live. Die. Live. Die. . . .

Like the petals plucked from a daisy, the moments fluttered by while my life hung in the balance, waiting for the final pull that would determine the outcome.

Live . . . die . . . live . . . and then slowly my lungs began to heal themselves. There was less mucus for the suction machine to suck up; tests on my blood gases also indicated that they were more normal. Those who stood watch knew that my lungs were beginning to recuperate from the damage of the toxins in the smoke. I began to breathe on my own, the vent of the respirator only giving me more oxygen than ordinary room air would have.

"How would you like to get that tube out of there?" This question, on the morning of January 11, seven days after the accident, came as a surprise. Three days earlier the swelling had begun going out of my face and eyes. Now, if my visitors stood in just the right place, I could see them again. At first it was a little like seeing "people . . . like trees walking around," reminding me of the blind man Jesus healed who needed a second touch to see rightly.[1]

I was about to get all excited about the prospect of talking again when the doctor cautioned me that it would take a little time for my voice to come back. Still, I was on the way.

36

"Take a big breath and hold it," he said. The anesthesiologist took hold of the tube, and it was out. I began swallowing. My throat felt strangely empty and more than a little sore. But, I did have a voice. A very hoarse, soft whisper of a voice. My mouth felt like thousands of troops had marched through it in stocking feet. Gene spooned a few small chips of ice into it. I don't remember anything ever feeling as good as the cool water trickling down my throat.

There was one small problem. The more my body began to recuperate, the more aware I was of pain. One of the first things I can remember a nurse telling Gene was, "We cannot give her enough drugs to take away the pain. All we can do is help her to cope."

In the past, burn victims have had to endure drug withdrawal, sometimes returning to the hospital just to overcome their addiction. The recovery period is so prolonged and the pain so intense, patients became unwitting drug addicts. To keep this from happening, morphine and Demoral were already being withdrawn from me and less addictive drugs substituted, but these were also far less effective.

With every passing day I became more aware of how badly I had been injured. I lay flat on my back because of the fractured vertebra. Two mattresses had been placed on my bed, the top mattress about twelve inches shorter at the head of the bed. I was positioned so that my head dropped off the top mattress to rest on the bottom one. My neck was constantly extended in an attempt to prevent contractures from forming as the burns healed, which would pull my chin down onto my chest.

Both of my arms were splinted and extended out from my sides, resting on foam-rubber cushions placed on top of two bedside tables. My feet were encased in huge plastic foam shoes. These "boots" were to prevent foot drop, which happens when the sole of the foot drops toward the mattress, resulting in a shortening of the leg tendons. In that position, suffering intense pain, I thought that I now knew what crucifixion must feel like.

Some have said to me, "I cannot imagine what it must be like to be burned that badly." They are right. No one can. Most people have only a nodding acquaintance with burns, maybe a bad case of sunburn or the result of contact with a hot burner on the stove or a curling iron or a match. None of these can prepare us for second- and third-degree burns, inflicted on a high percentage of the body surface.

Third-degree burns are referred to as full-thickness burns. When the skin is burned into the second layer (the dermis), the burn is third degree. Hair, nails, glands, blood vessels, and nerves have all been destroyed. With full-thickness burns, the skin loses its ability to regenerate itself and grafting is necessary for healing.

Because the nerves in my skin had been devastated, there was almost no initial pain—except in the areas of first-degree damage—so I was not completely aware of the extent of my burn injuries for some time. But the pain grew increasingly acute with each passing day.

There are no words to describe it. Excruciating. Insufferable. Fierce. Agonizing. Yes, and more. I began to wonder how much pain my body could endure. *Surely no more than today's pain,* I thought. But tomorrow would come and the pain was worse and the next day worse yet, and still, I lived. I learned that my body would not die from pain alone.

Dressing changes were the worst times. At first this was done in my room, and I would lie waiting, wondering when it would be my turn.

I could hear the metal utility cart loaded with supplies rattling down the hallway. Three nurses would enter my room, one of them pushing the cart. My door was then shut.

It was time.

The nurses opened packages of sterile gowns and put them over their green scrubs, the common uniform in the unit. With gloves and face masks in place, they opened package after package of sterile bandages. The sterile water splashed into the stainless steel pan, and I knew it was time to begin removing my bandages.

The bloody, encrusted wrappings were often stuck. But they had to be carefully, painstakingly removed, pulling open my burns. Just to have the wound exposed to air is painful, but, in addition, all the old ointments and the dead tissue had to be scrubbed off. I could hear the squishing sound of the sponges being rinsed. Over and over and over again each area was washed. Unimaginable pain. It felt as though my burns were being scraped with Chore Boy bronze cleaning sponges.

A brief pause as sterile gloves were changed told me enough debridement had been done, and it was time for the ointment to be reapplied. Usually Silvadene, a silver sulfadiazine ointment, was used. Sometimes the ointment burned; other times it didn't. But the mere touch of a gloved hand was enough to cause my raw nerve ends to scream.

At last the fresh bandages were wrapped around and around the clean arm. Left arm done. The same procedure would be followed until most of my body was wound in the white Kerlix bandages.

Then it was time for my bed to be changed. To enable the nurses to do this, I had to logroll from one side of my body to the other, putting pressure on my terribly painful arms, sides, ears, and face. Before it was all done, I had to get over what felt like a mountainous roll of fresh and soiled sheets, pads, and sometimes the foam pad the team called the "egg crate," because that is precisely what it resembled. The blue egg crate provided a softer resting place than lying on the ordinary mattress, taking the pressure off burns and preventing pressure sores from developing.

At last it was over. Then it was a toss-up: would the screaming pain of my body keep me awake? Or would the extreme exhaustion from enduring the change allow me to sleep? Gradually, the intense pain would begin to ebb . . . until the next dressing change . . . and the next . . . and the next. If I could have stopped these debridement sessions, obviously I would have. But the doctors knew better. Years ago, patients died because the burned tissue, which harbors bacteria under it, was not removed and the areas became infected. The wounds also need to be clean before unburned skin can be grafted onto them.

Life became nothing but pain. Time was the space between dressing changes. Mary, one of my nurses, would gently say as she finished: "There, that's one dressing change you will never have to go through again." At first it was small comfort, but it became a way of surviving.

But I wasn't at all sure I wanted to survive. Death became very alluring—quite beautiful, in fact, when seen as an escape from such pain. I already felt dead inside. I couldn't think anymore: couldn't remember my own address or phone number, the birthdays or ages of my children, or what day it was.

I can't remember making a conscious decision to do so, but I crawled more and more inside myself. For hours, I would stare into space, seeing nothing, hearing nothing. The television, turned on by one of the nurses, went unnoticed. Magazines and books lay untouched. At times I was very curious about this, wondering what was happening to me. Gene questioned me about the absence of my emotion: "Honey, you must feel so hurt, so angry about what has happened to you."

When my response was a bland, "I don't feel anything," he had difficulty accepting it, thinking that I was unwilling to face my own feelings. But even with his encouragement, I was powerless to stop my withdrawal. My world was reduced to pain, and I ran from it. My body had decided to reach for life, but I (the I that is really me) had not made that choice.

I remembered a little girl I had once known. Whenever her parents' voices had risen in anger, she would climb the attic steps to sit crouching in the dim light among the trunks, squirrel cage, baby bassinet, and cardboard boxes. She would pull up her knees and hide her eyes, covering her ears with her hands to block out the sounds coming from below. The little girl was me.

My dad was a strange mixture of a man. One summer day when I was quite young he came upon me, the littlest of his five daughters, sitting on the front stoop, watching the neighbor kids *whizz* past on their roller skates. He took my hand and walked down the street to the hardware store where he bought me a pair of my very own. Gifts were hard to come by in those early postdepression years, especially in a house with six growing children. It was a rare, spontaneous gesture.

His flaring temper was also spontaneous—but not so rare. The most unlikely incidents were capable of sending him into a rage. One day he brought home a packet of pins for my mother. When she did not respond with what he thought was an appropriate acknowledgment, a frightful argument resulted.

None of us ever knew what might set him off or who would bear the brunt of his anger. So each of us learned to cope in our own way. I learned to walk on "tiptoe" so as not to trigger his hairspring temper, feeling somehow responsible when it was unleashed. When the angry shouting would start, I had my own retreat—the attic. There I would sit, now and then tentatively uncovering my ears to test for sounds, scared and lonely. I didn't realize it at the time, but that is where I spoke some of my first prayers, as over and over and over I would say, "Make them stop. Please make them stop."

I liked the attic—maybe because it was all right to be scared there. It was, after all, a scary place. Fears had identities like dark cobwebs and the ever-present traps to catch any rodent invaders—not at all like the faceless fear that knots your stomach when you don't know who or what you're afraid of. Or maybe I liked the attic because of the aura of history, the security of the past when the present was unbearable. For whatever reason, it became my hiding place. I realize now that I have spent a good share of my life "hiding in the attic," scared and lonely and afraid to be me.

That January, faced with something too traumatic, too

painful, too overpoweringly frightening to comprehend, I climbed the stairs to my attic once more.

The nurses were painfully aware of my agony. They tried every way they knew to help me cope with my pain, told me all the little gimmicks other burn patients had used to get them through, thinking some of them might work for me.

I reasoned with myself. *You didn't holler and cry during dressing changes when the tube was down your throat; you couldn't. So why give in to that now? Be brave. Don't let it touch you,* I told myself.

I gave it a good try, but as the pain increased in intensity, I wound up tighter and tighter.

"It's all right to yell," the nurses would tell me. "It's all right to cry. It's better to let it out. Many burn patients end up with ulcers from the tension and trauma." To guard against this complication, Maalox, an antacid antiflatulent, was pushed on me with every meal.

On the morning of January 14, after a particularly grueling dressing change, Ernie, the assistant head nurse, gave me a coping tool. A good-looking young man with dark, curly hair and mustache, he reminded me a good deal of my own son. Perhaps that was the reason I felt such a closeness to him.

I was struggling, struggling too hard to get on top of the pain. Ernie began talking in a soft voice. "Relax. Just relax. Stop fighting and breathe smoothly and regularly."

"I can't," I said. "I am trying, but I can't."

He paid no attention to my protest. "Breathe in relaxation. . . . Breathe out pain and tension. Breathe in relaxation. . . . Breathe out pain and tension." Over and over and over he quietly repeated the phrases, until I found myself working with him, steadily, rhythmically breathing in and out.

"Breathe in relaxation. . . . Breathe out tension. Feel your feet and your ankles beginning to relax. Feel the muscles in the calves of your legs letting go. Relax the muscles in your thighs, feel them getting loose. And now the muscles of your hips and groin."

"Breathe in relaxation. . . . Breathe out tension." His voice crooned on and on, lulling me as he named each part of my body. Stomach and abdomen, lower back, upper back, rib cage, and chest. Shoulders and arms, wrists . . . hands . . . fingers. Neck and forehead, face and jaw. . . .

When I woke up, Ernie was gone; the shift had changed, and it was almost time for dinner. I had floated into a deep, peaceful, pain-free sleep, the first in days.

Naively, I had asked God to take away my pain. Others had prayed, thinking some miracle might end my suffering. But my pain was reality, a fact of life. My body was not created fireproof; it had literally been burned up. There was no escape from the physical pain. But, Ernie had shown me that the possibility of coping with it was within me.

This knowledge and the presence of a sheet of lined, legal-size paper pinned to a small bulletin board near me made bearing the pain possible. The hours of the day were listed down one side of the paper, each followed by a person's name. Our friends in First Baptist Church, Lebanon, had committed themselves to pray for me around the clock. Every time I saw it hanging there I was reminded of how many people were supporting me with their prayers.

Cards and letters had begun to arrive from places like Beaumont, Texas, and Billings, Montana; from Mt. Carmel, New York, and Van Nuys, California. They came from Baptists, Presbyterians, Lutherans, Methodists, and Catholics—some from people with no particular church relationship at all. But they had one thing in common: they were all praying for me. "We care about what's happened to you," they wrote. "We are praying for you. We love you."

There were those words again: "I love you." They washed over me, cooling the heat of the pain. Each evening, Gene would open the day's mail, reading the notes and names to me. "I pray for you at breakfast every morning." "A mass will be said for you daily for one year." "When I wake during the night, I think about you." Hundreds of cards came from all over the United States, until one day they filled three big cardboard cartons. Gene, who had started saving them for me at home in a small shoe box, was amazed. I was awed.

Yet, down someplace in the very core of me, a lot of questions were curled up like unborn fetuses. So many people were praying for my life, but I was praying to die. "Lead me gently home," I begged God repeatedly. They were asking for an end to my pain, but there was no end. Every day it grew more intense. Some, in an attempt to resolve their own questions, wrote answers to questions I could not yet ask. "God is testing your faith," many said. "He has something for you to learn from all this, some reason, some special plan in his mind."

"Maybe you are supposed to write a book about this experience." And one had taken time to write personally on an otherwise printed card: "Whom the Lord loveth, He chasteneth."

Those answers to unasked questions were the one thing I struck back at. Were they saying God had singled me out for the honor of being roasted like a hot dog? Did they intend to imply this was all part of some glorious master plan, which would be revealed to me in the sweet by-and-by? Testing my faith? Of course it was testing my faith. But was it a deliberate attempt by God to see how far I could be bent without breaking?

I lashed out at Gene when he read those parts. "That's crazy, insane thinking. God wouldn't. . . . He loves me."

Quietly Gene settled me down, and I placed those ideas in a box deep inside me labeled RAGE. I had no capacity to deal with them now. Later, perhaps. For now I would bask in the love that was shining on me from all sides.

I began to realize there was a power in this love. It was powerful enough to hold me up. In my mind I imagined a soft hammock woven out of the threads of all this love. I let myself fall ever so gently into it.

I felt supported by this hammock of love each time I logrolled onto my side (with no way to relieve the painful pressure on my arm) and looked at that yellow sheet of paper hanging there. I would think: *Someone is praying for me, right now. I can make it. One more roll over the hump in the middle of my bed and onto my left side as far as I can. Then the last burned areas on my back will be cleansed and redressed. Then all I have to do is roll onto my back and another dressing change is over. One more I never have to go through again.*

When my body was feeling on fire, I would imagine myself melting into this hammock. Later, this support was there in the hydrotherapy room, too. During those initial moments in the tank, when the bubble action was started and the water was moving over my body, I rested in the hammock. There was a sense of security in knowing this love would hold me up through the debridement and the scrutiny of the team of doctors and nurses who came to look me over.

I was not alone.

"If I make my bed in hell, behold, thou art there. . . . and thy right hand shall hold me" (Ps. 139: 8, 10).

5

Rub-a-Dub-Dub
One Woman in a Tub

After my initial encounter with the Hubbard tank when I was first admitted to the burn unit, ten days passed before I heard it mentioned again. My dressing changes and debridement had all been done in my bed, until my lungs had healed sufficiently to permit me to leave the respirator. Now that I was breathing on my own, I heard the nurses discussing how they might get me out of bed and transported to the hydrotherapy room, where the tank was located. Some technique had to be thought of to move me to the tank without bending my back, until the brace I had been fitted for arrived.

I was told I would be taken to the hydrotherapy room for tanking the next day. The image of the tank loomed monstrous in my mind. I lay awake most of that night rehearsing in my mind the hazy details of that first encounter.

In the morning, two nurses and two physical therapists tried to lift me onto the gurney cart by grabbing hold of my sheet, forming a sort of sling. I ended up on the gurney, but it was awkward and horribly uncomfortable. In a day or two, a better system was worked out. I would logroll onto my right side as far as possible while the plinth (the aluminum and plastic platform on which I rested in the tank) was shoved up against me. Then I was to roll over the aluminum

frame onto the plastic without bending my back. When I
was on it, the plinth was lifted onto the gurney.

That first morning I learned I was the only patient who
was wheeled into the tank room. So every morning from that
day on, I would lie still and tense, listening as the nurses
went in and out of the hydrotherapy room, caring for other
patients. Filled with a terrible dread, I waited to hear the
sound of the gurney bumping its way through the door. That
was my signal. They were coming for me; now it was my
turn. The process of getting my body onto the cart was
agonizing and the time spent in the tank tortuous.

Once inside the hydrotherapy room, I lay on the plinth
on the gurney while the bandages were removed layer by
layer. I felt as a newborn must feel once stripped of blankets
and clothes; its tiny arms begin to flail and small legs wildly
kick about. A piercing wail expresses the infant's feeling of
complete vulnerability. I was terrified to be completely
uncovered. My only security seemed to lie in my cocoon-
like wrappings.

When the last remaining covering was removed, the
plinth was secured at each end to a lift. I was swung up into
the air and over the tank, then lowered slowly toward the
water. There was a short halt—a pause in the mechanized
swing. That first day I thought I was going to slip off the
plinth. When that fear dissolved, I lay there poised above
the water, remembering how water feels on a burn.

A plastic sheet had been placed in the tank, lining it
inside and out as a guard against infection. It was filled to a
depth of about twenty-four inches with 100-degree water.
Salt and Betadine, an antibiotic, had been added.

The machine moved me gently into the warm water.
. . . Wonder of wonders, it didn't hurt. For just a few minutes
the water washed over me, soothing and relaxing. Then the
therapist began to debride, washing over each burned area.
I knew I couldn't stand the pain. I wished I could die . . . but,
I didn't. It is amazing what the human body can endure.

If there was any one thing that made the trip to the tank

and the bath any easier, it was Bill, one of the aides who assisted with the tankings. Big and strong, he would help me move, his powerful black arms holding onto the back of my head while I tried to get onto the plinth. He had a rolled-up sterile gown, which he put under my head to keep it out of the water. No matter how many times it slipped, he was there to fix it a little more comfortably. When the debridement was over, he made the transition from plinth to cart a little less painful. I would come to dread Bill's days off. The other nurses and aides could not match his strength.

This first day back in the tank I began to scream— inside. From then on, I screamed for months. But I would not let the screams come out, not here, not yet. Instead, I began to sing. And the nurses and therapists sang with me. The words that came out were, "*Do*, a deer, a female deer; *re*, a drop of golden sun. *Mi*, a name I call myself; *fa*, a long, long way to run. *So*, a needle pulling thread; *la*, a note to follow *so*. *Ti*, a drink with jam and bread, that will bring us back to *do-oh-oh-oh-oh*."

We sang other songs, some the nurses suggested, some I thought of. "Amazing Grace" was one hymn nearly everyone seemed to know, that and "Jesus Loves Me." Most of the words eluded me, even though Gene helped me make a list of familiar hymns, recalling lines for me. But, no matter how well rehearsed I was, they were difficult to remember once I was in the tank. If I had to think about the words, the effect just wasn't the same. So, I stuck with "*Do*, a deer," sometimes ending with a great crescendo. The more it hurt, the louder and more fiercely I sang. "*Do*, a deer, a feMALE DE E EEEEEEEEEEEEAHHHHHHH!" In that way I harnessed my screams to a song. Whenever I stopped singing, one of the nurses would pick up the refrain and others would urge, "Sing, Mary Ellen, come on."

Once when I remained silent a long time, one of them said, "You're not singing today."

"I think I lost my song," I replied through gritted teeth.

"Let's see. '*Do*, a deer—' " she sang to encourage me.

What kind of person can day after day inflict agonizing pain on another human being? What is the person like who routinely scrubs, scrapes, pulls, and cuts burned flesh from a screaming body?

In the past, burns that covered half the body were almost always fatal. Then new burn care techniques were developed, many of them for use on casualties of the Vietnam War. The new treatments greatly increased the chances of survival. Still, those who survive undergo great pain, and nurses must inflict much of the pain. Some last only a short time before asking for transfer to another ward.

What is the nurse like who stays on in the burn unit? Monstrous? Sadistic? Hostile?

"Sometimes I don't think I can take another day," Mary would tell me much later when I asked her how anyone could do what they have to do. "I wonder what my patients think about me when I am causing them such great pain. I look into their eyes and I can hardly stand it. I get through each debridement by picturing my patient walking out of the burn unit, healed."

In time, I would become familiar with the ominous pall that descended over the burn unit at least twice a day. Debridement and dressing changes were feared and dreaded by all of us and wearying and heart wrenching for the nurses. During those periods of time, the voices that drifted into my room sounded efficient and businesslike. Gone was the sudden burst of laughter that had become so familiar to me at other times of the day. Gone were the casual exchanges as nurses met in the hallway.

I learned later the nurses worked together in teams of two or three on the newer and more critically burned persons like myself. During the first few minutes of their shift, they chose which of the patients they would be primarily responsible for. This same block of time was used for "report"; the outgoing team briefed the relief team on the condition of each patient. Although they sort of "picked a patient," the RNs most experienced in burn technology tended to choose those of us who needed their expertise most.

There is some controversy over this practice, but it seems to be an advantage for the patient, since a nurse will pick a person she relates well to and to whom she gives better care. She may be more inclined to do "extras." However, with this system a nurse feels as if she is responsible for the patient twenty-four hours a day. When the patient walks out, it is extremely rewarding. But when the patient doesn't, it's like losing a member of the family.

Some of my dressing changes involved two or three hours of unrelieved work for my nurses and unrelenting pain for me. By choosing which patient they would care for, the work load and the tremendous pressure was shared.

The nurses did everything they could think of to make each painful dressing change a little easier. If quiet seemed to be an aid, they did their work in silence. If music helped, they scurried around looking for a radio. Country, rock, or easy listening, whatever seemed to soothe, was tuned in. WXTZ, the station I had listened to that fateful morning, became a bulwark, competing with the sounds of the monitors and warding off the emptiness of my room. It played twenty-four hours a day during my stay, becoming one of those few links with life outside.

Mary brought in her own cassette player so I could listen to the music from *Fiddler on the Roof*, when she discovered it was a favorite we shared. She also had with her a tape of hymns. In order to change tapes for me during a dressing change, she had to remove her gloves and put on a sterile pair each time the recorder stopped.

However much they would have liked to set their own pace for the debridement and choose their own system, the nursing teams always let me choose. Later, when I assumed some responsibility for my care, I wanted to have the worst areas done first and rewrapped before moving on. Doing it piecemeal like that took longer and was more work, but no one ever complained.

It would have been much easier for the nurses to keep me at a distance. So many of their patients died. Some were abusive. Some understood the necessity of the pain inflicted, but most didn't. How much simpler it would have been to remain cool and detached. Just do the job, change the dressings, check the IVs, take the blood samples and vital signs, suction the tubes, monitor the catheters. Instead they cared, and caring, they hurt.

In time their caring went far beyond my physical needs. Posters began to appear on my bulletin board and door: I Am Not Afraid of Tomorrow for I Have Seen Yesterday and I Love Today.

I'm OK. God Doesn't Make Junk.

Rita brought the first one. Later I found out she was hurting, too. You couldn't see her sore places as you could mine, but they were painful just the same.

Sharon would take time to rub lotion into my dry feet and to powder my sore bottom after a period of diarrhea. India would sit and read to me when she could have spent her free time in the lounge watching television or having a cigarette. Marie would always have some dumb joke that brought laughter to confront the screams. She and Ruthie would help me hold on to the funny side of life when it kept slipping through my fingers.

Each one brought years of training, but they also brought the gift of themselves. I learned about their families, their lives, and sometimes, their heartaches. When I heard of a baby shower for Becky and Lisa, I asked Gene to wrap two small pairs of booties and bring them to my room. They knew how disappointed I was to miss my daughter's shower, so they let me share theirs instead. The bits and pieces of themselves the nurses shared with me were like threads that held me to life when I wanted to let go.

I knew terror during my sojourn in the burn unit, but it was a fear of the pain itself, not of the people who inflicted so much of it. Back in the alley I had surrendered myself to the strangers who came to help me. Here it was no different.

I felt secure and protected in their hands. They valued the gift of my life at a time when I would have returned it as merchandise too badly damaged to be saved.

Wishard's Angels were in charge of me. I was in good hands.

> "God will put his angels in charge of
> you to protect you . . .
> They will hold you up with their hands
> to keep you from hurting . . ."

Psalm 91:11-12[2]

6

To Market, to Market
To Buy a Fat Pig

As the days passed and the pain increased when more of the burned skin was debrided, I drew almost completely inside myself. It was as if I had to protect "me" from the unbelievable horror my body was exposed to. Gene worried about the withdrawal almost as much as he did my burns. He was concerned that perhaps my brain had been injured or that irreparable psychological damage had been done. It frightened him to see the Mary Ellen he knew disappear, leaving a burned-out shell behind. And so he tried to coax me out with a game we had taught our children when outside circumstances became unbearable.

List Two Goods was the name of the game. The rules were simple: for every bad thing talked about, two goods about the situation must also be mentioned. We began our list together in a guest register booklet some friends from Evansville sent:

GOOD THINGS

January 4	Getting out of the burning building
January 8	Eyes opening so I could see
January 11	Getting tube out of throat
	Having ice-cold drink

January 23   Singing "Amazing Grace" in
             tank with nurses
January 26   Had Dairy Queen strawberry
             milk shake that Gene carried
             in

Our list included all the things, big and small, that brought joy into my day, and this became a chronology of my recovery. "Gifts came from a circle in Evansville." "Used the bedpan." "Logroll did not hurt as much." "Smelled Gene's shaving lotion as he bent to kiss me for the first time." "David Jans came to visit."

David had been critically burned himself seven years before when an asphalt truck he had been driving overturned, throwing him out into the boiling tar. He crawled through the boiling liquid, the heat searing deeper and deeper with every second of contact. Then he fought his way back to life through twenty-eight surgeries.

The day I was burned he heard the news report on his car radio and came almost immediately to the hospital, even though he did not know Gene or me personally. He and his wife, Mary, knew from experience what no one else could possibly imagine—exactly what Gene and I were going through and what was yet to come. During his first visit in the family waiting room, he had told Gene he would come whenever we needed him. And he did.

Seeing David walk into my room for the first time was like catching a glimpse into life after death and knowing everything was going to be all right. This handsome young man standing at the side of my bed had received third-degree burns over 62 percent of his body! He explained about the grafting that had been done, and showed me his hands, which, even though they were minus a few fingers, functioned incredibly well.

Mary came with him on one visit. She obviously loved David and was proud of what they had accomplished together. Intuitively she knew my unspoken fear. "People have a lot of questions about Dave and me. One person even dared to ask how I felt when he got undressed. So, I told him. WHOOOPEE!"

What Mary didn't know was that I had never felt good enough for my husband, even when I had been physically attractive. I had been fourteen, going on eighteen, as they sometimes say, when Gene graduated in midterm from Bay View High School and left for Northern Seminary. I was convinced in my own mind that I would never be able to "hold on to him."

Gene's mother had done little to enhance my confidence. She saw me as a barrier to her dreams for Gene and was determined to break us up. Besides, Gene had been dating the daughter of some family friends who more nearly fit her picture of his future wife. Privately I thought she was probably right. *I'm not good enough for him.* My family wasn't religious like his; we weren't "in" at the church. And I was, I felt, just a dumb, little, high school girl chasing after a college man.

Yet, on a cold, dreary November day, I had knelt beside a very shy, self-conscious young man and we committed ourselves to each other for better or worse. Gene's mother and father had moved to Oregon in the summer. We told them we wanted to be married before they left. But Gene would not be twenty-one until the end of October that year and needed his parents' signature to marry. In what was, perhaps, a last-ditch effort to save her son's future, his mother had refused to sign. Only Jan, Gene's sister, had returned to Milwaukee to be at our wedding. But neither the rain outside nor his parents' absence had more than momentarily dimmed my happiness. Kneeling there, holding Gene's hand, I had admitted to God that I wasn't much—maybe there was someone who could love him better, but no one could love him more.

I had feared then and for years after we were married that someone more "right" for him would eventually take him away from me. Or, even worse, he would realize his mistake, but be too kind or too professionally harnessed to say so.

When Gene was called to the First Baptist Church in Lafayette, Indiana, as assistant pastor, I had felt fairly comfortable. There was a pastor's wife in the church, so the expectations for me would be few. But whenever I had been asked to participate in some way, I had ventured forth with fear and trembling. My inner anxieties built up as the time drew near. I would experience nausea and sweat profusely. When desserts were served just before I was to speak, I dropped silverware, spilled tea, and in every way felt clumsy and stupid. Away from the security of my home and family, I was a duck out of water.

Despite my discomfort, what I did came off fairly well. But I had never been able to accept the affirmation that followed. I discounted it as people merely being polite. Each time I would vow not to get myself into that kind of situation again, knowing all the time I would, because that was what it meant to be a good wife to Gene. I would retreat into my "attic," hide myself behind Gene and the children, salving my wounds by telling myself, *A woman's place is in the home anyway.*

Sometimes the kids and I would go with Gene to training conferences and lab schools. He would be involved all day and evening in some training event, either participating himself or, later on, giving leadership. The children loved every minute of the quiet times we spent in the woods or beside the lake; they still talk with excitement about their neat vacations at Green Lake, where the American Baptist conference center is located.

But I felt as if I were standing outside in a snowstorm, looking in the window at a group of people having a great time around a crackling fire. Nobody even knew I was out there. If someone did notice and invite me in, I was ill at ease. I knew I didn't belong with these people; they were professionals.

The fact that some of these professionals happened to

be women had let out another of my dragons, the green one. From time to time I had been sucked under with waves of jealousy. I had never known when it might strike—or who would be involved: women Gene counseled with, his secretaries, or, as in these cases, women he met at conferences. I was certain, as I'd heard my father say so many times, "Any woman can get any man if she tries hard enough."

Those years held an insidious insecurity that plagued what in every other way was a profoundly satisfying relationship. The more I watched Gene grow in his vocation as a minister, the greater my fear became. I had never been able to figure out why a man like Gene wanted to marry a klutz like me.

Now my physical attractiveness was gone. Because I was still struggling just to exist, I had not allowed myself to face what would happen to our marriage if I lived the rest of my life disfigured. Unconsciously I filed that thought away, still unable to face the reality of my present condition.

By January 21 my lungs had improved enough to allow me to have surgery. It was beautiful! For almost one entire day I was unconscious. No pain! And while I was under the anesthetic large areas of my body were completely debrided painlessly. Many burn victims without lung damage and a smaller percentage of burns have a major portion of their debridement done in this way and much earlier in their treatment.

When I woke up back in my own room, Ernie began to lay temporary grafts over the freshly cleaned areas until I was well enough for areas of my own unburned skin to be removed and placed on the damaged areas. Later I learned that a burn patient's best friend is not a dog, but a pig. The pigskin laid on my body until my own skin could be harvested for grafting brought with it some immediate relief from the unrelenting pain. Ernie laughed as he urged me to look at my new skin. I took one hesitating peek. My little pig was obviously a spotted one and now I wore his coat.

Some burn units do have skin banks, and Wishard is in the process of developing one. The skin is harvested from cadaver donors with the consent of the family. The requirements are less constricting than for a kidney or cornea donor, but many families are reluctant to consent, feeling that their loved one's body is maimed. Actually only a slight discoloration is noticed, and skin is only taken from areas covered by clothes. Cadaver skin is the best temporary wound coverage known at present, though a very successful artificial skin, a blend of powdered shark cartilage and collagen (a major component of skin), has been recently developed at MIT and Massachusetts General Hospital. Unfortunately, it is years away from wide use.

One week later, I returned to surgery for more debridement. I went eagerly this time, having experienced the bliss of one painless day and knowing now that more pigskin would soon cover the exposed areas. I didn't realize it then, but the worst of the pain was behind me now that the major debridement was complete.

After what seemed an interminably long time of lying flat on my back, unable to sit up to eat, and trying to logroll ever so carefully so as not to bend my back in the slightest, my back brace arrived on January 30. What a horrible contraption it was! Made of padded metal and leather straps, it fit me like a dog harness. It took just about every member of the morning shift and me to figure out how to get into it while still resting on my back. As bad as it was, it was my passport to getting out of bed and back on my feet.

Later that afternoon I was strapped onto a tilt table. Because I had lain flat for so long, it was necessary to raise me by degrees. Slowly, cautiously, the tilt table lifted me to a vertical position. I was able to take the ascent well and was soon in a standing position, although still strapped to the table. I saw my room in its entirety for the first time. And when the nurse pushed me out into the hall, I was amazed at the new perspective I gained. I had thought the unit was circular so that sometimes the nurses were around on the far side where they couldn't hear me if I called them. Although a special call button had been rigged up so I could push it with my foot, quite often I didn't get it back in place and I would have to rely on my weak voice to get help. Seeing that the nurses were just down the hall a short distance gave me a new feeling of security.

Much to my amazement, the next day when it came time to try my legs, I found I had forgotten how to sit up. It may sound strange, but I had to consciously rethink the pattern of movements necessary to get myself up on the side of the bed. With a lot of help, I was up, my head and body feeling like they were suffering from an acute hangover. The floor seemed miles away from my feet. Finally, with a nurse holding me up under each arm, I took two faltering steps and collapsed into my wheelchair.

I was light-headed and weak. The new position put unaccustomed pressure on my burns. The back brace was cumbersome and hard. Yet, despite all the discomfort, I was proud of my accomplishment. That day I knew I was going to survive.

7

Blindman's Buff

"**O**pen your eyes, Mary Ellen." How many times had a nurse said those words to me? At first, it was their way of knowing I was conscious and capable of responding to outside stimuli. Later, it became a way of urging me to look at myself.

It had been frightening to be unable to open my own eyes those first days in the hospital. But now, long after the swelling had receded, I chose to keep my eyes shut a good deal of the time. There is something about shutting out the visual that helps us cope. How many people watch an injection being given to themselves or a blood sample drawn? The most natural thing is to turn the head away, avert the eye.

"Shut your eyes. Don't look," I would advise my children as I washed a scraped knee and applied a Band-Aid. They would scrunch up their eyes and stop crying. Following my own good suggestion, I steadfastly refused to look at my burns. During every dressing change or tanking, my eyes remained tightly closed.

I soon found many opinions among the doctors and nurses about the value of a burn victim seeing herself. "Open your eyes," some urged me. "You need to see yourself and begin to accept what's happened." Others warned me, "If you don't see how it is now, you won't be able to recognize improvement."

One day when I was on exhibit in the tank, surrounded on all sides by doctors, residents, interns, junior medical students, therapists, aides, and nurses, Dr. Yamaguchi pressed me hard to open my eyes and look at myself.

Suddenly, almost vehemently, Carolyn, the head nurse, said, "You don't have to look, Mary Ellen. Wait until you're ready."

I appreciated her coming to my defense. There was one thing I knew. Whether good for me or bad, my eyes must remain shut. Perhaps I was only bluffing myself, but I could not look. If I did, I knew I would start screaming and never stop.

When I finally did take my first look through barely half-opened eyes, I wished I hadn't. I was lying flat on my back in the tank, holding up my left arm for the therapist to scrub. As she paused to give the sponge a quick rinse, I opened my eyes just a crack.

It was more than I was prepared to deal with. My arm looked like a piece of chopped meat at the grocery counter. I could see where the escharotomy had been performed down the entire length of the arm. During my first night in the hospital, my fingers and left arm had been surgically cut in order to prevent the skin from bursting open (much as a too-long-roasted hot dog will do) and to prevent the swelling from cutting off circulation, jeopardizing the limb. I had been aware of what was happening, but I hadn't thought much about it. Now, the opening in my arm looked like the Grand Canyon.

Up until that time, the worst cut I had ever seen was on Jeff's arm the day he fell through our storm door. It gaped open and bled a great deal. But the skin was there intact. When carefully stitched back together, it didn't look awful at all. This was different. My skin was gone, burned off, and in its place was this mess of red. My hand, stuck off the end of my arm, looked weird and grotesque; the fingers shriveled and curled up like plastic melted out of shape in an incinerator.

Even when I was entirely wrapped in Kerlix, I could still see the percutaneous pins projecting out the ends of each finger on my right hand, which was probably the most severely burned area. Some tendon removal had been done and the pins had been inserted in an attempt to keep the fingers in a good position.

Later that night I told the nurse, "Mary, I looked at my left arm in the tank today."

She waited, saying nothing.

"It was awful. It looked gross."

In the nurses' notes for that day she wrote, "Patient looked at arm today." I wonder what would have been written if she could have seen the turmoil going on inside me. A more accurate statement would have been: "Patient looked at left arm today and became nauseated by its grossness." I knew I had been right. The less I saw of my burns, the better I would be inside.

Some of the nurses still continued to encourage me to look at myself. They believed that I must see what I looked like and begin to accept that I would never be the same again. In a sense, they were right. It is a step that must be taken. But I hadn't learned to crawl yet. It wasn't time to walk. I knew that.

I think they knew it, too, because one morning almost a month after the accident, one of the nurses suggested, "You really should look at yourself. You look so much better and you still have beautiful eyes."

I relented. "OK," I said, "bring me a mirror. I'll look."

But she never returned with the mirror. No matter how much the nursing team urged me forward, they never pushed. They always seemed to know when I had simply acquiesced and when I was truly ready to move on.

When Gene came to feed me dinner that evening, I announced my intention to look at my face: "Where did you put that little mirror? Did you take it home?"

He made a great pretense of hunting for the mirror through the few personal things in the room, all the while asking, "Are you sure you want to do this?"

No, I wasn't at all sure, but I guessed it had to be done. Sooner or later, I had to know.

He held the mirror in his hand, still hesitating. "I'd better go ask the nurse if it's all right." He was afraid and I knew it.

A few moments later he came back to the room and offered me the little mirror. Ironically it had a picture of Ziggy and Put on a Happy Face printed on it.

It is a strange experience to glance into a mirror expecting to see the reflection you've grown accustomed to for over forty-six years and instead see a strange-looking person staring back. There were bandages wrapped around the sides of my face and over the top of my head. My eyes, nose, and mouth were exposed. At least, I guessed they were mine. The eyebrows and lashes were gone; the nose was raw in places, scabby in others, and still swollen. The lips were thick and covered with a peeling crust. It wasn't me. It couldn't be!

There were no tears. No loud outbursts. There were feelings—such feelings. But I couldn't look at them any more than I would look at my face again for a long, long time. Instead I took the feelings and quietly packed them in my rage box.

Before Gene left the hospital that night, I asked him to bring a picture of me when he returned. I told him which one—a picture of the two of us taken at Jill's wedding. I referred to it as our silver wedding anniversary picture. One doesn't get many photos that are truly pleasing, but this picture was. I felt it would help me hold onto the image I still thought of as me. It seemed important to me that the nurses know that I hadn't always looked ugly and deformed. I had been pretty. I needed to remember that, too.

The following afternoon I saw myself reflected in the mirror of my grandson's eyes. It seemed like only yesterday when we had all gathered together to celebrate the first birthday of our first grandchild, Jeff's son.

The decision to let Jeremy visit me had been easily made. Even before his birth, over one year ago, I had been surprised by the stirring in me as I sewed the cover for his bassinet. As I cared for him and played with him after he was born, I realized that this child was somehow miraculously my own. Jeremy Lawrence Ton became a continuation of the love Gene and I shared. How I wanted to feel his warm, wiggly little body against my own again!

The nurses had assured me each time I asked them that I could not give any infection to Jeremy. I felt so unclean, like the lepers I had read about in the Bible, as though any contact with me would somehow contaminate the baby. But I was soon told that I was more likely to be infected by Jeremy.

The next day, I sat in my wheelchair as a nurse completely draped me in a white sheet and put one of their funny caps on my head. Then Gene wheeled me down the hall and through the double doors separating the burn unit from the rest of the corridor. Vicki and Jeff would bring Jeremy to this small area where visitors were required to wash their hands and don the sterile gowns. My mind was full of questions: *Would he know me? What would he think? Would he be afraid of me?*

As we came toward him, Jeremy was busily unpacking his diaper bag, strewing Pampers, toys, and containers of powder and lotion on the floor of the small waiting area. I waited until he noticed us before I spoke to him. "Hi, Jeremy!" I said in the soft, weak voice that was now mine.

He stood back, holding onto his mother, his face solemn, his already round eyes wider. He was quite still as he saw this strange creature in the chair on wheels. "It's grandma, Jeremy." Both Vicki and Jeff tried to encourage him.

Gene stooped down, and Jeremy toddled over to him on newfound walking legs. His smiling face reflected his eagerness to get to his grandpa. From the safety of Gene's arms, he curiously looked me over.

"He's afraid," I said disappointedly. "Don't force him. Just let him take as much time as he needs."

Everyone assured me he wasn't afraid; he would be all right. But as Gene pushed me back to my room, all I could see were those two, big round eyes. I understood how different I must look, swathed in bandages and sheets, and he was just a baby. But this was the first time someone I knew and loved had looked at me and didn't recognize me. It hurt. For the first time since the accident, I realized I didn't look like me any longer.

Later, after Gene had gone and the nurses finished yet another dressing change, warm tears ran down into my bandages. I remembered what Jane, the charge nurse on second shift, had said to me after I had gotten a little feisty with Gene one afternoon. "Mary Ellen, you are never going to be the same again. You will be a different person physically, mentally, and emotionally. You need to begin to accept that."

I had been so angry. How could she say something like that to me? When Gene came back and I told him about the incident, I had angrily protested through my tears, "I'm me, I'm me, I'm still me."

But after seeing Jeremy today, I wondered—was I? Was Jane trying to help me begin to deal with truth? Was I wrong? My own grandchild didn't know me. My brief glance into the small mirror had been frightening. It was true: no one could identify what lay in my bed from any slides or photographs of Mary Ellen Ton.

But I was still not healed, I reasoned. When I was well again, everything would be all right. It was just a matter of time.

And so I entered into the grief process so graphically defined by Elizabeth Kuebler-Ross. I began to grieve the loss of my appearance as I vehemently denied that any permanent damage had been done. I recalled other burns I had suffered: the octagonal red sore that appeared on the arm of a little girl who had pressed against the temperature control of an old-fashioned oven, burns on my fingers from hot irons and stubborn stove racks. I tried to remember each one: how they had sometimes formed scabs, how they were sometimes slow in healing, and how the scar had looked after they had been healed. There had been no visible trace of a single one of them.

I would be just fine, I comforted myself. I would just continue to pray to God for my complete healing. . . . I would be just fine. . . .

8

A Skin to Wrap
The Baby Bunting In

My first skin grafting surgery was scheduled for February 5. The miracle of skin grafting escaped me at first, since I could see it as only a release from pain. As grafts are laid over the prepared areas, the pain decreases dramatically.

With the exception of the outer skin of my left thigh, my legs had not been burned. My abdominal area was also relatively free of burns. My skin was harvested from these two areas to cover the full-thickness burns on my hands, arms, shoulders, and face.

During this first surgery, a split thickness of my skin was removed with a dermatome, a special surgical instrument for this purpose. I always envision a meat slicer in a butcher shop when I think of this procedure, although I have never seen this instrument. Some of my harvested skin was put through a mesher, which stretched it so a smaller donor tissue could cover a larger burned area. Skin put through the mesher does not make a nice, smooth graft. I have come to refer to it as my chicken skin.

Those areas above my knees left untouched by the fire took on their own scars as they loaned skin to other parts of my body. From my knees to the very top of my head, I will forever bear the fingerprints of the monster fire. With one exception. The new ten-dollar bra I was so concerned about

67

did its job of protecting me before it was destroyed. Thanks to Warner's, there is an almost perfect outline of a bra on my body.

Later in my room, my own skin, which had been harvested in the surgery, was also placed on my right cheek, left cheek, forehead, and jaw. The grafts were all stapled in place, the sight of which sent shivers up and down my spine.

It was a source of wonderment to me that two persons had volunteered to give me skin. This is no small thing, since it requires major surgery and involves pain and permanent scarring. My sister, Hallie, and Glen Gossage, a friend of Gene's, both offered this rare gift. However, donor skin is only taken from living persons in rare instances (where identical twins are involved or a few other peculiar circumstances), so my own skin was used.

Skin grafting is really quite miraculous when you stop to think about it. Normal healthy skin is taken from one part of the body and laid over the destroyed skin, bringing healing and wholeness to the other part. The donor site itself becomes painful and scarred while the burned area ceases to hurt and receives new life. What a parable to illustrate 1 Corinthians 12! What an image for Christians to emulate!

> . . . God has so adjusted the body, giving
> the greater honor to the inferior part, that
> there may be no discord in the body, but that
> the members may have the same care for
> one another. If one member suffers, all suf-
> fer together; if one member is honored, all
> rejoice together (vv. 24-26).

I had an almost 100 percent take of the first grafts. Not all burn patients are so fortunate. But some other complications developed after the surgery. During one of the operating procedures a catheter was placed in the femoral artery (in the inner thigh), and a blood clot developed as a result. I was started on Coumadin therapy (a blood thinner) and was once again confined to bed, this time for two weeks.

I had been ambulatory for three days between the time my brace had been fitted on January 30 and the day before this first surgery for grafting on February 5. Although walking was extremely painful, it had also been an accomplishment. To find myself immobile again was a big disappointment.

"I feel like I'm going backwards," I confided to Gene. My left leg was propped up on three pillows, my head still fell off the edge of the top mattress, and my arms were still extended out to the sides, except for meals. And worse yet, I was being basted. The new grafts had to be kept constantly moist by applying sterile water through the bandages at least once every shift.

It was miserable being soaked. The cold water chilled my entire body. When the nurses tried warming the water, it got too hot and scared me.

"First I was roasted by the fire and now they are basting me," I complained as Gene tried to offer what encouragement he could. He was discouraged himself with this new setback.

But in addition to being roasted and basted, I was also being stuffed. A lot of calories are required by the body to grow new skin. It was crucial that my food intake be monitored carefully. I was supposed to have 4,000 calories each day. That was more than twice what I normally consumed. Always weight conscious, my big fantasy had been to have a doctor tell me to eat and eat and eat. Now it was no longer a dream. I was brought three huge meals a day and special loaded-with-calories milk shakes were served in between.

But now that I was supposed to eat all I had ever wanted and then some, I couldn't eat at all. Food lost its appeal. There was texture but no taste. Even when I first woke up in the morning, I felt as if I had just finished a Thanksgiving meal. All night a "burn unit special" milk shake was propped up next to my head. All I had to do was turn my face slightly and suck on the straw. In the end, I couldn't eat anywhere near the total 4,000 calories. So, back went the tubes. All day and all night, the goopy-looking white stuff dripped through a nose tube into my body.

"I don't want to live, Gene. When I have my next surgery, pray with me that I will never wake up."

He prayed with me, but not for death. Each of us had been praying in our own way and time, but not together. Now each night before he left, he touched me wherever he could—on my foot or the top of my head or gently laid his finger on my lips—and we cried out our despair to God together. We also began to thank God for the "flowers along the way," all the little things that graced our days and kept the flickering candle of hope from completely extinguishing.

On those nights, as Gene bent over me, I could imagine rather than feel the rough texture of his suit coat against my cheek. I took deep, deep breaths of the faint lingering fragrances of Irish Spring and English Leather that still clung to him. It was like listening to a favorite love song, stirring memories both longingly sad and intimately beautiful.

On February 14, Heidi, the occupational therapist for the burn unit, brought me a small, nickel valentine and pinned it on my bulletin board. Gene came later in the day. In a small box he had to open for me was a gold necklace with a tiny little teddy bear hanging on it. At that very moment a sad-looking, bedraggled little teddy bear was sitting on a shelf in our living room next to a framed excerpt from *The Velveteen Rabbit*.[2] Long ago a small boy named Gene had played with it and loved it. Today it is almost hairless and its eyes and nose have been replaced with bits of embroidery floss.

Gene had given me his teddy bear when I was still in high school and he went away to college. In the custom of teenaged girls, I had propped it on my bed all day and laid it on my pillow at night. Later when I had carried Gene's babies, the little bear exactly fit the hollow place in my back that ached so badly when I tried to sleep.

Now Gene didn't say a word; he didn't have to. I knew he was affirming the meaning our history held for him. And I remembered how it all had begun one cold December night in 1947.

My mother and I were doing dishes and talking to my brother, Chuck, who sat on a stool watching. (Boys didn't have to do dishes in our house. That was women's work.) When the telephone rang, Chuck lazily moved to answer it, coming back to announce that Gene Ton wanted to talk to me.

"To me?" I asked incredulously. "Why does he want to talk to me?" Gene was my brother's friend. Gene had called our house often to talk to Chuck, but not to me.

When I overcame my astonishment enough to pick up the phone, Gene invited me to Youth for Christ. At that time, he was the president of the Baptist Youth Fellowship and one of his jobs was to round up the troops for the Saturday night meetings of Youth for Christ. He was a pretty shy guy in those days and not at all my type. Besides, I wasn't sure I wanted to give up my baby-sitting money for that evening. I had learned long ago how to hide behind a lot of bravado. I tried it out on him as I said, "You mean with the gang, or with you?"

Gene had stuttered and stammered a little and then said, "I mean with me."

The name of the preacher and what he said that night have long since faded from my mind. But I have never forgotten the strange, new stirrings that began within me, or that I responded to the preacher's message by walking down the aisle with Gene at my side.

It's a long walk from downtown Milwaukee, where the Youth for Christ meeting was held, to our home in the Bay View area on the south side. Gene had a lot of time to share his dreams and plans. As he talked about becoming a minister, pastoring a church, I felt a magnetic excitement. From that night on, there had never seemed to be any question that his dream would become mine.

In a small group I attended once, I was asked to draw my spiritual journey using symbols to help interpret major events. As I thought of that Youth for Christ meeting, I drew a road sign with an arrow designating a sharp corner ahead. Although I had not fully realized it at that time, I turned onto a road that would determine the rest of my life.

In January, when Gene left for college, we carried on a long-distance courtship. There had been no money for weekend trips home, and in those days, long-distance calls were for emergencies. So we had drawn the blueprint for our life together in long, daily letters: what our homelife would be like (there would be no arguing, ever); how many children we would have; and on and on. I had believed that somewhere, waiting in the wings, was my fairy godmother who would touch me with her magic wand at the right moment and turn me into a minister's wife.

My life had already begun to revolve around Gene: his school vacations, semester breaks, and too-short summers. Even his God had become my God, as he shared his developing thoughts and faith. It wasn't until years later that I realized I didn't know what *my* faith consisted of. I had known by heart what Gene thought about God and could quote my husband accurately, beginning with "Gene says . . ." or "Your father thinks . . . ." His faith had been a good one and it had held up well for a long time, but it wasn't mine.

I knew, as Gene held the oblong box so I could see the little gold bear, that he, too, had been walking backwards into the past. I was pleased that he seemed as eager to share his valentine as I was to share mine.

Several days earlier I had asked our pastor, Dr. McKenney, to help me make a valentine for Gene. If he thought it was silly, I never knew. He had acted like it was a most important task as he hunted for a piece of paper, scissors, and a red pen. I had given a lot of thought to the words and who would help me. I dictated and he wrote:

Our yesterdays,
Memories, happy and sad.
Our todays
Awesome and frightening.
Oh, but our tomorrows,
Love our tomorrows.

Dr. Mac had cut the paper into a heart shape and hidden it in a book from which Gene retrieved the valentine as I directed him. It was a beautiful warm moment. A little gold teddy bear and a scrap-paper valentine—two such little things.

There were other little things, too—a small foil packet of Avon perfume impregnated on a paper tissue that was enclosed in a valentine sent by a friend from our church in Evansville. I couldn't have the perfume rubbed onto me, but Gene held the tissue under my nose as I breathed deeply the lovely fragrance. Burned people don't smell very good. In fact, I stunk. It was such a little thing.

One of the little things I received weighed only seven and one-half pounds. "Gene just called," a nurse named Lonnie said as he came into my room about 12:30 one night late in February to announce the gift's arrival. "Jill's had her baby. Everything is fine."

When Gene came by the next day during visiting hours, I heard all about our second grandson, Jeffrey Owen: his weight, his length, and that his birth had been recorded on film. Bill had been in the delivery room and, with the doctor's permission, had photographed Jeffrey's arrival. Later I delighted in the pictures and others Gene took when he went alone to meet our second little grandson a few days later. At seven and one-half pounds, Jeff-O was just a little thing, but his coming was another link to life, and I began to look forward to watching him grow.

And then there were the gifts of my son Joe, a strong, silent guy. I still enjoy telling the story of how when Joe was just a little boy I would feel his sudden tug on my skirt. If I didn't kneel down to his height, another tug would soon follow. When we met at eye level he would put his small arms around my neck and say, "I love you, mama." That was, of course, my cue to say, "And I love you, my Joey." It was one of our important rituals for a number of years.

As he grew to his teens and it became too embarrassing to be serious about the expression, we turned it into another type of game. I would grab him roughly and croon, "Mama's baby." He would gently shake me off, but not before he had a good hug.

Now, this affectionate boy-turned-into-man gave me the magic words again. He never left my bedside without saying, "I love you, mom." He and Janet made many trips from Evansville to spend a few self-conscious minutes in my hospital room. They were expensive trips for two kids on a tight budget and it was not easy visiting me. Janet's own mother had died when she was eleven so it brought back painful memories to her. But come they did: Joe, in his cowboy boots, looking grossly uncomfortable in the yellow gown worn backwards, and Janet, her lovely soft eyes filled with tears.

We touched with our eyes. We touched with our words. But, oh, how we did need to touch physically. One of the hardest parts of being so badly burned is being untouchable. Just to feel the warmth of a hand on my skin! There seemed to be no place to touch without causing pain and presenting the danger of infection. Then, one day, as Joe and Janet were leaving my room I raised one of my big bandaged paws and waved to get their attention. With a great deal of effort, I bumped my foot against the sheet at the bottom of the bed. As they received my message they began to loosen the sheet until my right foot stuck out. My right foot had no burns and no needles. As it wiggled free it was grabbed and given a big squeeze and then a rub and then a nice pat.

Sometimes you feel things clear down to the tips of your toes. And sometimes your toes send messages clear up to the center of your heart. Oh, the pure joy of the touch of a human hand that signaled not pain but peace and love! I think that there were never five toes as loved as mine.

The excerpt from *The Velveteen Rabbit* came to me, not so carefully typed, from another son. Not all of my children can easily find the words to set their feelings free. Jack found himself locked into an event that needed words, yet he had none of his own. What he sent me spoke with greater clarity than if he had written volumes.

He had copied Margery Williams's words exactly as I had typed and framed them to sit on the shelf next to Gene's little bear. At the very point in my life when I most needed to hear the affirmation made by the old Skin Horse, the words came to me from my "wordless" son.

> "What is REAL?" asked the Rabbit one day. "Does it mean having things that buzz inside you and a stick-out handle?"
> "REAL isn't how you are made," said the Skin Horse. "It's a thing that happens to you. When a child loves you for a long, long time, not just to play with, but REALLY loves you, then you become REAL. It doesn't happen all at once. You become. It takes a long time. Generally, by the time you are REAL, most of your hair has been loved off, and your eyes drop out and you get loose in the joints and very shabby. But these things don't matter at all, because once you are REAL you can't be ugly, except to people who don't understand."[3]

Imagine what those words communicated to me as I lay there swathed in blood-soaked bandages, lips swollen and burned almost crisp, no hair to speak of, my eyes only a slit, giving off an odor offensive even to me. It was my firstborn son saying: "I love you, mom. You are not ugly to me. You are REAL." Many people said it using many different words, but no one has said it better.

After the two-week stint in bed waiting for the blood clot to dissolve, I began to improve rapidly. The sharpness of the pain was abating and I could walk more easily. I relished the day I was able to walk down the hall and into the bathroom alone. Privacy was a precious commodity.

The remaining debridement of scabs and crusts had been postponed because of the Coumadin therapy, since there was a greater risk of uncontrollable bleeding than of infection. Much healing had taken place by now, so dressing changes were neither as prolonged nor as painful. Another grafting, which would probably take care of the remaining areas, was set for February 25.

But as Dr. Yamaguchi stood next to my bed one morning before the appointed day, he said, "I cannot operate on you—not if you don't want to live."

Either Gene or the nurses must have been talking to him, I reasoned.

"Your attitude is important to the outcome," he continued. "I can't take that responsibility."

This man had worked hard to save my life. It must have hurt him to think I was unappreciative of the gift he had helped to give me. So I told him our plan, Gene's and mine.

"Each time I think about dying, I try to get a picture of driving up our street and turning into the driveway in our bright red Camaro. I *do* want to go home."

Although expressing a wish to die is not at all uncommon for a victim of severe burns, it is never treated lightly. It was crucial to me as a patient, and to Dr. Yamaguchi as my surgeon, that I affirm some spark of a will to fight for life. After I had given him that assurance and he had carefully monitored my attitude in the next few days, he agreed to operate on February 25.

The surgery went well and there was a good take. Not

so good as the first time, but the grafts that I lost were in place long enough to halt more pain, and some of the underlying tissue began to regenerate itself.

Still I felt a tremendous amount of anxiety about being touched in any way. It hurt. Whenever anyone simply walked into my room, an automatic defense system tightened my body. But, Heidi was soft, gentle and soft, like a furry kitten. Her voice was quiet and soothing, her touch gentle, her movements slow and nonthreatening.

Each day she worked every part of my hands, the PIP's, DIP's, M.P.'s. (She had a secret code, too.) All I knew was, nothing moved. "Pull, pull, pull," Heidi would say. I pulled, but nothing happened.

My favorite exercise was extending my arms out to the side. This was painful, but not too difficult since I rested that way in bed. While my arms were extended, I slowly swayed my upper body back and forth in the wheelchair.

"I'm flying," I told Heidi. She stood in front of me, her arms extended, and flew with me.

I was afraid as Heidi worked with my hands and there was so little progress. Scary images of being permanently handicapped kept chasing me around the room. But I could escape them when I "flew." I felt like Jonathan Livingston Seagull and imagined flying right out of that room over green trees, blue sky, and foamy seas.

Heidi's and the other nurses' tenderness and care, my family's love and encouragement, these were the still small voices that God used to speak to me . . . after the fire.

9

Home Again, Home Again, Jiggity Jig

My cocoon was being taken away. Since the day of my latest surgery, February 25, more and larger parts of me were being left uncovered. I was healing. At least that's what the nurses told me. But as I sat slumped over in my wheelchair, too weak to sit up straight, scarcely able to pull myself up out of it, I didn't feel healed. I didn't look healed, either.

The arms, sticking out of my hospital gown, looked foreign to me. I couldn't seem to make myself realize they were my arms, my hands. They looked like someone had dumped dirty paint water down on them—brownish red, deep purple, dark gray where small parts of the last grafts were dying. And where the grafts had taken, the skin was hard and bumpy.

They didn't feel like my arms, either. Instead they were stiff, heavy, and wooden, and I couldn't tell where they were. Sometimes, lying in bed, I thought they were resting across my chest. When I tried to move them, I realized they were actually still extended out on the bedside tables or had fallen down beside me.

I longed to have my bandages back in place. They hid the reality of what had happened to my body, and I didn't want to deal with it.

When my son Jeff or Gene came to visit, I could tell by the way they both avoided looking at my arms and hands that they were appalled by what they saw. I don't know what we had expected, but certainly not this. We all refused to talk about it, clutching instead at what the nurses had said so often: "You can't tell what the burns will finally look like until at least twelve months after the injury." In time, we realized that we had read far more into those words than was ever intended. But, for the present, they became something to hide behind, like a big box in the attic. I crawled behind that box, thinking soon the bad and scary things would go away and I could go back downstairs untouched.

I didn't realize that the real bad and scary things were packed inside me—my feelings. The anger, bitterness, and fear. The questions: *Why did this happen? Why me? Where was God?* All the things that in time would hurt me more than the fire were with me all the time and I didn't even know it.

Maybe that's why the words I listened to one morning late in February had so little effect. "You'll be ready to go home soon." Rita was doing my dressing change at the time.

I offered no response. I wasn't prepared to. Besides, when was soon? I had adjusted to my new home and had blocked out any thoughts of when I might get out.

"You don't believe me, do you?"

It wasn't so much that I didn't believe her as that I wasn't ready to deal with it. Even when the nurses on the next shift again mentioned it, I refused to admit that I might be going home soon. My skin still had lots of open areas. I was barely able to make it down the hall to the toilet and shower. My body was painfully sore to touch and the parts didn't work right: my legs wouldn't lift me off a chair, my arms were pulled up in front of me as if to ward off an attack, and my hands were useless.

For the next few days it appeared the nurses had launched a Convince-Mary Ellen-She's-Going-Home campaign. Almost to a one, they breezed into my room and said, "I hear you're going home."

Still not convinced, I asked Mary, my night nurse, late one afternoon. "Everyone says I'm going home. What do they mean? Like, how soon?"

"Two, maybe three weeks," she answered. "You're filling in really well now."

"But I have so many open areas yet," I protested. "They won't all be healed that soon, will they?"

"Maybe," she said, "but we've sent patients home with open areas."

I couldn't believe it! In the back of my mind, tucked away where it couldn't get to be too big a thing, I had hoped to be home by Easter. But this was the end of February. Two or three weeks would make it March.

"March 21st," Marie guessed. Someone else said March 10, and then the doctor said March 14.

The push was on. Get Mary Ellen ready to go home. No more bedpan at night. I never imagined that would be bad news. But it was. Due to so much catheterizing, when the need arose, it had to be attended to pronto. It was all I could manage in the daytime to get out of the wheelchair, down the hall, and open the heavy door to the bathroom. But during the night? It was difficult to get out of bed and it meant calling a nurse to first get me untied from all my apparatus and then wrap my legs in ace bandages. I knew I'd never make it. When I tried to argue with them, I was told, "You won't have a bedpan at home."

When Heidi, my occupational therapist, told me, "Tomorrow have Gene bring some clothes; you're going to learn to dress yourself," it sounded ludicrous. I could scarcely manage to handle a spoon, couldn't pick up a glass, or open a milk carton. How could I manage the intricacies of buttons, snaps, and zippers?

But, patiently and insistently, they pushed back my physical boundaries. I was proud of each new accomplishment, like a small child balancing precariously on a ledge. And childlike, I wanted to shout, "Look at me! See what I can do!"

Gene was equally busy at home. He cut off two boxes to the exact height necessary, so my arms could be extended on them when they were placed on each side of a twin bed. An old chair was brought down from the storage space over the garage so I could sit on it in the shower. A hand-held shower head was installed and push-button phones ordered. We talked about what chair could be padded for me to sit in, and how I would manage when his week's vacation was over, leaving me alone during the day. Having been well indoctrinated about the risks of infection, he scrubbed down my entire bathroom and hung a sign on the door: Mary Ellen's Bathroom. No one else was to use it.

Gene was very worried about his ability to do a dressing change, though the remaining unhealed areas were few and relatively small. The nurses suggested he come in one morning and observe this new and somewhat frightening responsibility: removing the dressings, standing guard as I showered to offer assistance when necessary, applying fresh ointment, and covering the burns. Watching the nurse go through this procedure was a breeze, but we both knew that doing it ourselves would be a whole new ball game and we were scared.

Still, Gene was as excited and joyous as he was when we brought our new babies home from the hospital. His enthusiasm was infectious, and I was soon caught up in it.

Early on going-home morning, Ernie came in to get me ready. He packed a lot of the odds and ends of bandages and ointments, thermometers and wash basins, splints and my egg-crate mattress. Then he said, "Get dressed."

Just like that!

He must have seen the dumbfounded look in my eye, because he added, "Call me if you need me."

One of the key phrases in the burn unit was, "Have you tried?" It was their way of pushing against today's limitations. To every "I can't," came a firm, "Have you tried? Have you tried *today*?" Had any one of them been willing to accept yesterday's accomplishments as tomorrow's goals, I would not have dressed myself that day. I got my clothes on, somewhat twisted, untucked where they should be tucked, but on—except for my shoes. It was impossible for me to bend to get my shoes, so Ernie put them on and tied them.

With underpants cutting into tender skin, no bra, a blouse and half-zippered skirt, compression hose I wore night and day up over my knees to control swelling, I waited for Gene, exhausted from the effort expended in putting on just a few clothes and wondering how I could handle all that would be a part of going home.

Later I wondered if Gene was as nervous as I was as I cautiously edged my way into the car. It was a little like the sudden awareness of complete responsibility that clobbers new parents as they leave the hospital with their newborn. It would certainly test the mettle of this man who had undertaken my care. The worst he had handled in raising four children was the bucket brigade when they upchucked. It was I who had stood by while a stomach was pumped after an aspirin overdose; I who rode to the emergency room holding sanitary napkins to gaping, bleeding wounds; I who held a little boy down while a doctor put in stitches without anesthesia when the novocaine had failed to work. It was I who handled soaring fevers, convulsions, and cries in the night. It was all in a mother's day.

Could he take care of my open burns? It was a test of trust. I felt I should have a big sign printed in red letters stuck on my back: Fragile. Handle with Care!

After what seemed an interminably long ride, we made the left turn onto Sixty-third Street. I could read our street sign: Sunset Lane. A turn to the right and now I could see the fire hydrant that stood like a gatekeeper beside our driveway.

My house. My home. How many times during the last two and one-half months had I pictured that house in my mind! The black and green squares I had so patiently painted on the garage door were a reminder of a happy September Gene and I had shared together scraping and repainting trim. My violets, dressed in finest purple, seemed to be watching for my arrival out of the dining room window. I swallowed hard and blinked back the tears of joy. I was home!

Gene parked the car in the driveway and came around to my side to help me out. I moved like an old, old lady. There was no place to either push or pull me without touching newly healed and still painful skin. Once out, I made quite a show of determinedly walking up the short pathway by myself.

"Are you OK?" Gene worried.

"I'm fine," I proudly replied. Whereupon I sank to my knees trying to make the one small step up onto the porch.

Neither of us had given a thought to the fact that I hadn't navigated steps since the day of the fire. Now I had merely raised one foot up, slowly following with the other, and my knees had folded. There I was kneeling on the stoop, hollering, "Don't touch me, don't touch me," to Gene as he ran to my side.

All of my bravado spilled out. *I knew I couldn't handle it,* I thought. I had been specially warned that a fall could start a hemorrhage while I was taking Coumadin, the blood thinner. I was frightened to think of that happening and yet embarrassed. After all, the neighbors were probably all watching my big return home. I had been the klutz again.

"How are you going to get up if I don't help you?" Gene asked, bending over me.

"I don't know. I don't know. But don't touch me."

"Let me help you, Mary."

"No, it will hurt. I can do it myself."

But there was no way I could get up alone. Gene finally lifted me up under my right arm, amid my protesting ouches. It was the beginning of a new pattern of relationship; Gene trying so hard to help me make all the adjustments to being home, and me giving voice to all the pain I felt free to express with him.

But for the moment nothing mattered. I was home. I

wandered through each room looking at all the familiar pieces of furniture, the pictures, the bric-a-brac, the books—all the treasured things that made our home different than any other, that made it our own. I had left all these things in their place that Friday morning in what seemed to be another lifetime.

I had thought it would feel like coming home after a vacation: carrying in the luggage, unpacking, cozying-in, and knowing there is no place like home. But instead, I felt like a stranger here.

I didn't realize it then, but homecoming is the beginning of the birth process. This time, instead of laboring to give birth, I would labor hard and long to be born again. For over seventy days I had been in the womb of a burn unit, growing a new and strange-looking body. I was not at all sure I was ready to be so abruptly forced into the birth canal.

Jane was right: I was not the same person. In fact, I did not feel like a person at all, just a body. Thick, black crusts covered my face and upper arms and shoulders. Hard, alligatorlike skin grew on my arms and hands where grafts had been made from my upper legs and abdomen. Pieces of my ears were burned off; misshapen fingers scarcely looked human and certainly didn't do human-type work, and my eyes pulled down into a monster face. This body was weak and frail and full of pain.

I sat slumped in a chair, propped up with pillows, too tired from the short trip home to move while Gene fixed lunch. Everything was wrong! Everything was backwards! I was the fixer of lunches. I was the one who put pretty place mats on the table, placed a plant or candle in the middle, arranged his plate, asked him what he wanted to drink, and called him to lunch.

How could I sit at the table with him? I, who had always brushed my hair and put on fresh lipstick and sometimes even changed clothes, just to look nice for my husband. How could I make my way into the kitchen now with my hair all but burned off, my lips thick with dried, peeling skin, wearing a dumpy, stained housecoat?

In the confines of Wishard Hospital, it was all right to be burned and repulsive to look at. I was closed off from the rest of the world in the small burn unit, seen only by the nurses, doctors, and therapists who were trained to treat badly burned persons. No visitors were allowed in the area except my immediate family. All my needs were attended to: someone cut my food into bite-size pieces, milk cartons were opened, plastic coverings on the silverware were removed.

My therapist had cut a piece of foam tubing, which was slid over the handle of my spoon, so I could manage to precariously hold it in my palm. When I used the toilet, a professional was close by to care for my hygiene. Someone was always available to open a door or drawer, take a cap off a toothpaste tube, adjust the volume on the radio, or turn the impossible knobs on the television.

They didn't even think I looked bad. They had seen me from the very beginning; to them the process of healing was miraculously beautiful. At first when one of the nurses would say to me, "You look great! You look beautiful," I cringed inside, feeling as though I was being mimicked. But by looking into their eyes and faces I soon came to know that to them I was indeed beautiful. They looked at a healed burn victim through special and unique eyes.

To be suddenly thrust out of my cloistered world that Friday was like finding myself stark naked in the harsh, cruel glare of a blinding spotlight. I wanted to cover myself, to hide, to run away. I longed to just evaporate. So I again retreated to my hiding place deep inside myself. With each humiliating experience, I backed further into that private attic of mine.

In the hospital I had repeatedly said to Gene: "I look so ugly." Sitting slouched at the lunch table propped up with pillows my first day at home, I felt ugly. My fingers were covered with crusty scabs and stuck out from the end of arms that were stiff and sore and hurt badly when I lifted the spoon to my lips. My face ached and cracked open each time I opened my mouth. I scooped at my food, pushing it off my plate, dropping it down my front, and leaving a mess around my mouth.

My plastic cup had an oval piece cut out of it, starting at the rim and extending two inches toward the base. It looked as though someone might have grabbed it and broken a section out. This opening allowed me to stick my thumb inside the cup. Pinching the wall of the cup between my thumb and index finger, using my left palm for additional support, I could lift it to drink—and slobber. I wondered what Gene was thinking as he sat across from me. I knew I was gross looking. How long could he hold up under this? What was going to be left of our marriage?

We had decided to sleep in the guest room where there were twin beds. We couldn't even lie side by side, much less get close to each other. If Gene even sat on the side of my bed, my body suffered shock and pain from the movement. Several times every night I had to wake him up to escort me to the bathroom. My arms were encased in sleeping splints, making it impossible for me to take care of myself. Gene sat on the edge of the tub patiently waiting while I sat on the toilet and then . . . he cleansed me. I felt sick inside each time. But, what could I do? There was no escape from the humiliation.

On Saturday, Jill and Bill came bringing little Jeffrey. He was three weeks old, and this would be my first glimpse of him. Now I could hold him and nuzzle him in his tiny neck. Very gently Jill laid her baby in my arms. It was a very special moment for a mother and daughter to share.

But I began to rattle, "It's OK, he can't get anything from me. I know I look awful, but I'm not 'catching.' " Even as Jill assured me she wasn't in the least concerned, I knew it had to be terribly hard to lay that new little baby in my lap and watch as my scabby finger reached out to touch his soft cheek.

The weight of his seven pounds on my arm and upper

legs was enough to hurt and break open an old wound. I looked down and saw the bright red blood stain spreading on Jeff-O's fleecy white blanket. "Jill, you better take him. Look what I've done. If you use peroxide on it right away, it should all come out."

"It's OK, mom. It doesn't matter," Jill tried to soothe me.

But it did matter! Jeffrey was several months old before I held him again.

All that Saturday I knew something was wrong. We had been carefully instructed to watch for any abnormal bleeding because I was on Coumadin. At first I only suspected there was blood in my urine, but every trip to the bathroom made it increasingly evident. I didn't want to tell Gene. I was afraid he would insist I return to Wishard. Besides, I didn't want to spoil Jill's and Bill's visit; it was the first time I had seen them in such a long time. Then, too, I felt responsible. I was convinced that I had done the damage when I fell on the porch.

So, all day Saturday I refused to let anyone know I was in trouble. But by Sunday morning I knew I couldn't put off telling Gene any longer. He did exactly what I knew he would do—called the burn unit to alert them and bundled me into the car for the trip back. I was sure they would keep me there, but instead I just had another blood test done and received a shot of Vitamin K.

But the condition did not improve and by Tuesday I was in a lot of pain. Gene knew I was having some discomfort, but I had not told him how badly I really felt. So when our minister came to call, we sat cozily around in the living room as though he had simply dropped by for tea. I sat in the chair Gene had draped with an old blanket to protect it from stains. For months I could be tracked through the house by the trail of blood spots, scabs, and dried skin I left behind me. Dr. McKenney talked briefly with me about how I was feeling, and mentioned the valentine he had helped me make. Then, he and Gene fell into conversation.

Their words droned all around me like a bothersome fly. The pain was clutching and clawing at my stomach. It didn't even occur to me to say I was miserable—months of suffering pain had conditioned me to retreat inside myself.

At last Gene's eyes met mine and he knew immediately I was in distress. He jumped up and hastily ended the visit with Dr. McKenney.

I didn't even argue when he said he was going to take me back to the hospital. I knew I needed help. The pain was so intense by the time we arrived that I was conscious only of the effort to place one foot in front of the other in order to move myself forward.

There is no place in the burn unit except for the resident burn patients. This brought some confusion as they debated what to do with me. I was wrapped in one of the yellow hospital gowns—right over my coat and all—and quickly escorted back to the hydrotherapy room, which was not in use at this time of day. My friend, Mary, was on duty, and she stayed with me, helping me to undress and make the climb up onto the gurney to lie down since there were no beds in the tank room.

There followed such a procession of doctors as even I had never seen. I was certain every specialist on the staff came to poke, press, and probe my middle. The final diagnosis was internal hemorrhaging, caused by the drug Coumadin. But it was 10:00 at night before the shot I begged for was at last administered and I felt myself getting sleepy. The pain was bad enough, but the hurt over being hospitalized again after such a brief respite was too much. I pleaded with Gene to stay with me until I went to sleep. He sat holding my hand while I grew drowsier and drowsier, opening my eyes occasionally to mumble, "Don't go. I'm not asleep yet."

Later, I learned that two male patients had been moved into one room so I could be readmitted to the burn unit. I think they must have known how important it was to my emotional health to be where I felt secure, since it was stretching the rules to allow me to come back there.

Once the Coumadin was stopped, I improved quickly. I was back to twice daily blood tests, and in need of a transfusion because my blood count had dropped so low. As soon as that was done, I would be able to go home again. But there was no blood to match mine. Apparently some antibodies had built up during the last several months, and the hospital could not locate a match for me. On Friday they sent me home with my promise to return as an outpatient for the blood transfusion and to keep moving to guard against clotting, a danger now that the blood thinner had been stopped.

I kept my promise. Before Gene left for the office, he turned Channel 13 on for me. Every half-hour commercial break, I struggled up out of my chair and walked the circle from the den through the hall to the living room, dining room, kitchen, utility room, and back to the den. I often wondered during those strolls where I would have gone if our house hadn't been built with a circular floor plan.

The pattern of our day was soon set. Before Gene left for work he fixed breakfast for both of us and prepared a plate for my lunch. Then he did my dressing change, and I flopped (carefully) into my padded chair in the den. All day long I intermittently stared at the boob tube, dozed, and stumbled around the house on my exercise jaunts.

With one exception. On Wednesdays I was to report to the outpatient clinic to be checked. I had been the kind of person who changed clothes to go to the grocery store. Now I didn't own any clothes that fit me because I had lost over twenty pounds during my days in the hospital. One would think my clothes would hang on me. Wrong! I looked five months pregnant; the waistbands on my skirts and pants missed coming together by a good three inches.

I had to borrow some of Jill's maternity pants. What a strange-looking figure I was walking through the halls of Regenstrief Clinic. Stooped shoulders, hands stuck out in front as though to feel my way, face covered with scabs and dressings, trying to hide inside the hood pulled forward over my head.

As I walked, I would catch a glimpse of a person turning to someone beside them to make a quick exchange. Then the informed and informant would both take a look. Small children who had strayed from their mothers hurried to the safety of a familiar side and clutched hand. Did a woman think I was deaf as well as burned when she uttered, "My God, look at that woman!"

I heard and I saw and I died.

Now that I had been taken off the Coumadin, the scabs and crusts were to be removed from my face and hands. Before that time there was danger that the resulting bleeding could not be stopped. The procedure of placing wet cloths on the crusts to soften them for more easy removal was begun in the hospital. Gene and I tried to work on it at home, but it was a gruesome thing. Even with the soaks, they only came off tiny bit by tiny bit. As soon as one small spot was clean, it bled and oozed and built up an even bigger crust. It seemed the harder we worked, the worse the situation became. My shoulders and upper arms began to break open again and the scabs came off newly healed places, leaving them raw and oozing. These were not the hard, black crusts I had come home with. They were a yellowish brown, moist and pussy. The constant seeping caused them to grow larger until some of them hung down over my eyes. At dinner one evening I had tried to conceal my grossness by bending my head toward my plate. As I did, a huge hunk of the pus-covered crust fell into my food! The sight of the scab on my plate was the proverbial last straw.

Gene was exhausted and so was I. And we were both scared to death.

In the clinic the next day, Dr. Smith told us I had a staph infection. My whole face, shoulders, and arms needed to be debrided right away. He had Carolyn come over from the burn unit to take care of it. Carolyn interceded on my behalf, asking Dr. Smith why I couldn't go home and soak them off with Gene's help. But the doctor was insistent that it be done immediately. He knew I was angry, but he also knew what was best for me.

I sat precariously perched on the edge of the examining table, like a nervous bird about to take flight, while Carolyn made the necessary preparations. She tore open packages of sterile gauze pads, in anticipation of the expected bleeding, and a suture removal pack containing surgical tweezers and scissors. I closed my eyes, again playing my game of blind-man's buff. Gene was nervous and fidgety. I noticed before shutting my eyes that he had moved as far away from the table as he could get in the small examining room.

Without any soaks to soften them, without benefit of any pain pill, every scab and crust was pulled off my body with the tweezers. Carolyn started on one side of my face and began working her way around. I knew where each crusty scab was and so followed her progress in my mind. Each area took on its own pain as it was ripped open. I could feel a warm trickle as my blood ran down my face, or arm, or chest. Carolyn kept up a steady stream of chatter, talking first to me and then to Gene, who was noticeably frightened by this, his first exposure to debridement.

The work of a burn nurse is tough. So are the decisions of the doctor. One look at Gene and I had told him neither of us was in any shape to handle that job ourselves. When it was over and the last dressing had been applied, Gene and I both felt like a huge weight had been lifted from us.

When both Gene and Carolyn left the room, Dr. Smith talked to me about the need to find someone I could talk to about my feelings. The depression I thought I was covering up so well was quite apparent to him. He suggested the mental health clinic at Wishard, pastoral counseling, and drugs to cope with the extreme depression I was exhibiting. But I still believed Gene and I could handle everything ourselves.

It wasn't until later that night when Gene tried to change my dressings that we realized we had handled all we could on our own. He tried to wash the areas newly uncovered in the clinic. Gently, gently he worked trying to remove the Silvadene ointment. But it wouldn't come off—not gently! He tried a little harder, and I cried out in pain. Of course, he stopped. "What do the nurses do when it hurts?" he asked me.

"They say, 'I know that must hurt,' or 'I'm sorry,' and keep right on scrubbing."

"Mary, I can't."

"I know, Gene, I know. It's all right. Do the best you can, and I'll try not to let you know when it hurts. Tomorrow we'll call for the nursing service."

Even before I had come home from the hospital, nursing care or household help had been suggested to us. But the open areas were insignificant then, and we felt sure we could make it on our own. This, however, was something else. My entire face was a mass of raw, open, oozing sores; my shoulders and arms were breaking down more every day, and Gene was fatigued. Keeping up with his demanding job and running the house on top of the anxiety of my care were taking its toll. He was completely worn out. I could see it in his eyes and face, and instead of crying alone, he cried a lot with me now.

In a way, I was like a child. I knew we needed professional help, knew I needed a trained nurse's care. But, I also was aware of their tough love. They wouldn't stop when it hurt, or let a bit of Silvadene remain just because it was too hard to get off, or allow me to skip "just this one dressing change," as Gene did.

It was a real serendipity when we contacted Upjohn Healthcare Services and discovered that two of the burn unit nurses moonlighted for them. Once again I was in the hands of my angels from Wishard. Marinel and Edie began to come twice a day, alternating according to their hospital schedules. They accepted the job, assuming it would last for a couple of weeks. None of us had any idea I would need nursing care until the end of June.

   Just as it would begin to look like the end was in sight, I would develop another infection and the skin would break down all over again. Three times we went that route, and each time I sank deeper into depression. It was such a helpless, hopeless existence. Inside me a woman was screaming just as the woman who had clung to a window ledge that fateful day had screamed, "Help, help, somebody, help me." My rage box was crammed full. The lid was about to blow.

10

Down in the Valley,
The Valley So Low

•

Gene had gone out for the evening. About eight o'clock I walked into my bathroom for some Kleenex to wipe away my tears. Lately the tears would start as soon as he left the house. I could manage to hold onto my feelings most of the time he was home, but let him walk out the door and they came rushing out in dry, racking sobs. With the tissue in hand, I dabbed at my eyes and awkwardly tried to blow my nose, all the while looking at my reflection in the large mirror.

Contorted by crying, my face appeared even more grotesque than usual. Bits of Xeroform, a petrolatum dressing that kept crusts from forming again, clung to the infected areas; the medication in the dressing, warmed by my own body heat, ran into my hair, plastering it to my head in dark, greasy patches. My mouth twisted even more out of shape as I opened it wide, the contractures from the scarring on either side pulling at it cruelly. The tight scars tugged at my bottom eyelid, exposing more of the fiery red lining. I was overwhelmed with horror at my own reflection. I could find no sense of identity in that image. It could not possibly be me. Without any warning, the rage so long boxed up inside me burst out. I screamed . . . and screamed . . . and screamed. The intensity of my screaming broke open some barely healed places on my face, and the blood trickled down over my eyes and cheeks.

"Monster. Monster. Ugly monster," I shouted at the horror-movie character looking back at me. It was true. Hollywood used makeup to create the image I had become. Did the plot call for terrifying the victim? Open a door, pull back a curtain, run through the rainy night, and come face-to-face with a horrible-looking creature with scarred and disfigured features.

Making strange guttural noises that aptly complied with my monsterlike appearance, I eased myself back into my chair in the den. Beautiful women paraded across the screen of my television set, a constant reminder of my own physical unattractiveness. Appealing young women with flawless features, soft hands, and tanned smooth bodies; lovely women closer to my own age tauntingly asking, "Can you guess my age? I'm forty-one!" Pretty older women, displaying lovely hands, wistfully complaining, "What's a woman to do about these ugly brown spots?"

This particular night a documentary film was being aired. It told the story of three women of different ages and racial backgrounds who had undergone mastectomies. Once I had believed this to be the most awful thing that could possibly happen to a woman. It's funny how old boogeymen are chased away as new ones come to take their places.

"You dummies. You silly, stupid women," I shouted out loud to the gorgeous blonde in her Danskin disco dress, to the black woman with perfectly smooth, delicately brown skin. "You're still beautiful. All you have is one small area of scar tissue, easily hidden with your clothes. No one will ever know what's happened to you unless you choose to tell them. No one will ever look at you and stare as if you were some kind of freak."

This was not my night to be sensitive to the personal trauma of the women involved. I was too enmeshed in my own drama. When Gene came home, I spewed out my anger to him. My rage box was opened.

The itching had become intolerable. One of the side effects of healed burns is dry, scaly skin, which seems to itch unceasingly in varying degrees. Any slight amount of scratching is apt to break open the delicate skin, leaving more open areas to heal. There were times when it felt as though hundreds of small bugs were creeping over my body, and times when a thousand mosquito bites couldn't have itched any more. The nights seemed to be the worst. I would wake from a sound sleep with my entire body furiously itching.

Lying there as long as I could, I tried not to move my body against the sheets. Unable to tolerate it for very long, I would get up to get the pill that had been prescribed to help control the itching. Gene had laid it out for me on the desk so I could pick the tablet up by touching the end of my tongue to it. I was unable to pick up such a small object even without my sleeping splints on. To me this was one more sign that I wasn't a person any longer but rather an animal sticking its muzzle out to get its food.

By that time, the frantic noises I made in the throes of the itching wakened Gene, and he would gently apply the Nivea cream to my skin. It was the only legitimate reason for rubbing; I begged him to go over and over the worst areas. It was a toss-up whether the pain of being touched or the relief of being gently massaged would win out. At last Gene would try to convince me to lie back down. He would sit on the edge of my bed softly speaking the words of the relaxation exercise Ernie had taught me. "Breathe in relaxation. . . . Breathe out pain and itching. . . ." And then again, "Breathe in relaxation. . . . Breathe out pain and itching." The metronome of his tired voice quietly tried to beat back the savage pounding.

Sometimes it worked, and I dropped fitfully to sleep only to be awakened a short time later as the ants were crawling again. When all else failed, I would reel crazily round and round the house in search of some relief.

It was on one such night in early May, a short time after

the floodgate had been forced open by my screams, that I began my wrestling match with God. The itching had been bad all day, and now there seemed to be nothing to give me much needed rest. The pills had no effect; the lotion burned instead of soothing. Gene was so exhausted he had stopped waking up to help me hours earlier. On one of my circular frantic dances, I began to scream out to God.

"I hate you, God. Do you hear me? I hate you for letting this happen to me. How could you? Do you even hear? Do you even care? I hate you."

I felt so lost . . . so betrayed . . . so abandoned. I was amazed at the sudden fury of my attack. I had thought I was handling the situation in a somewhat calm and reasonable manner. The questions friends had tried to answer for me in their own way, I hadn't even asked. All my feelings of outrage had been carefully tucked away, hidden so well I didn't even know they were there. Now I joined the legion of "Why?" askers. Why would God, whom I loved and trusted, betray me in this way?

I felt very much like the woman, married twenty-five years, who had given her life to a man and his dreams—shaping her life in his mold, keeping his house and bearing his children, loving him, idolizing him—and then discovered he had betrayed her faithfulness with another woman. I experienced the same hurt, the same rejection, the same agony of betrayal. I had loved God. I had given him my life. I had used my gifts and talents in an attempt to share him with others. I had read to learn more about him, practiced spiritual disciplines; I had grown in my relationship to him and felt I really knew him. And now? How could he allow this to happen to me if he had loved me in return?

I remembered how people had written about my accident. "God has a reason," they had said. "God has some lessons to teach you." Could this horrible thing actually be a part of some diabolical plot deliberately executed by God as part of his overall plan for me? Is this what I must believe and accept? I could not love such a God.

Was God punishing me for something, as some said? I laid out each of my failures and shortcomings, like cards in a game of solitaire, every sin and transgression I could ever remember committing, and turned them over one by one. It was an ugly sight—my immature dependence on Gene, my critical spirit, the jealousy I had never really struggled to outgrow, my failure to be all that I could have been to Jill during her tormented teen years. Then there was my refusal to give up my own feelings in order to help Gene through his own private hell and the person I needed to forgive but couldn't or wouldn't. But, even when all of my failures were laid out on the table in front of me, I could find nothing that merited this kind of reproach from God. It was undeserved. Unfair.

"God saved your life," others told me. "He saved you from the fire because he has some work yet for you to do." I had been willing, although sometimes reluctant, to try anything I felt God's inner urging to do. But, surely, whatever I had left to accomplish was not going to be enhanced by my scarred and crippled body. Besides, if God had moved to save me from the fire that day, he was a little late. Of what use was my life as it was now?

I could have died. Indeed, by all reasoning I should have died. Even the statistics were against me. (A patient's mortality rate can be roughly determined by simply adding age to percentage burns. In my case, 46 plus 55. Statistically, my chances had been nil.) I had even prayed to die. "Please, please, lead me gently home. Please, Father." Countless times I had spoken those very words into his ear.

If God was interested in answering prayers, he was listening to other people's prayers for me to recover instead of mine. "We are praying for you," the cards, letters, and telegrams had stated. There were more of them and only one of me. Maybe God kept a tally card. Was that why three other persons died in the burn unit while I was a patient there—not enough little marks on their cards?

I seemed to sink further into despair with every passing

day. I couldn't stand myself. My body became a prison. Locked inside, I scratched and clawed frantically trying to escape. But there was no escape—I was trapped forever in this monster's body, more animal than human. Some of my family had been concerned about my mind when I had retreated inside myself in the hospital. Now I began to wonder, too. I couldn't make my mind think straight—I would read and not remember, start to talk and forget what I had been going to say; watch television and not know what I had seen. I was frightened by my own body and afraid that my mind had been damaged, too.

I closed my eyes, trying to shut out the ugliness of my world. But I knew there was only one way to shut it out permanently. I had thought about it for days. I would simply go to sleep . . . and not wake up.

One day, after my dressing change had been completed and Edie had gone, I fell asleep in my chair in the den as I usually did after a painful session. I woke with a dreadful feeling in my stomach. As so often happened upon waking from a deep sleep, the impact of the fire seemed to slam into me with incredible force. Each time it was like reliving that moment when in one horrible instant my whole body was devastated.

I don't remember thinking, *I am going to end it all right now*. I just found myself searching for my car keys. They weren't on top of Gene's bureau or my dresser. They weren't on the desk, either. They were hanging on the key rack beside the kitchen door into the garage. Gene had probably placed them there after retrieving them from the fire. It seemed strange to think that those keys had gone through the fire, too, but they were unmarked. They were also out of my present reach.

I used my foot to inch the step stool out of the utility room, across the kitchen, and over to the door. Balancing myself with my hip and arm against the refrigerator, I stepped up on the stool and batted at the keys. They fell to the floor.

I had fallen too many times trying to bend over to risk it now on the hard kitchen floor, so I kicked the keys to the dining room door, and on into the living room, until they were beside the couch. Carefully lowering myself onto the couch, I reached again for the keys. Finally, I laid down, dropped my arm off the edge of the couch and managed to get my thumb through the ring holding the keys.

Back in the kitchen, I laid the keys on the counter nearest the door into the garage. Using the palms of both hands, I turned the doorknob and stepped into the garage.

But no matter how I tried, my fingers could not manage to pull the handle that would release the car door. I stood beside the car and cried out my despair and frustration. I felt utterly defeated.

Most of that night I lay awake thinking about what I had almost done. I was amazed at how calmly I could contemplate my own death. It even seemed the reasonable thing to do. I could not understand why I was alive like this.

The next day I went out into the garage again and tried to open the car door until the pain of my body overcame the pain of my soul and I gave up. For many days after that I tried unsuccessfully to get into the car, but it was an exercise that only added to my feelings of helplessness and loneliness.

How could I make Gene understand what it was like? How could I tell him that I wanted to end my own life? I tried to voice my pain and only bitterness was heard.

"Why, after being roasted like a human hot dog, did those nurses and doctors fight so hard to save my life? Why save a charcoal-broiled body when my soul has died?"

Gene's eyes filled with tears. "I don't know how to help you, Mary. I want to make it better for you, I want to take it away, but I can't. I'm glad you're here. . . . I'm glad you're alive."

"But you don't have to live like this, Gene. Yesterday I went out into the garage with every intention of ending it. I couldn't even open the car door, much less turn on the ignition. I can't live and I can't die. What do you call this?"

"Oh, babe," he moaned.

"Please don't call me that. Don't ever call me that again. I'm not your 'babe' anymore and won't ever be again."

"I just want to help you. Somehow let you know I care. . . . I love you. We can make it through this together. We have to take it one day at a time."

"You really want to help me? Then help me die. All you'd have to do is open the car door, turn on the ignition, and go to work. It wouldn't be you doing it, it'd be me. Please, Gene. If you love me, you won't make me live like this."

"Mary, Mary, I can't do that. If I could just hold you in my arms and somehow comfort you. I can't even reach out and touch you. Does this hurt too much?" he asked as he knelt on the floor beside my chair and ever so gently laid his head on my knees.

"No, it's all right. It doesn't hurt. But, it doesn't change anything, either." I laid my ugly, bent hand on his head. It was the first tender moment we had shared in months.

There was release from the tremendous anxiety of the moment in the warm tears that streamed down both of our cheeks.

> We must walk this lonesome valley,
> We have to walk it by ourselves,
> Oh, nobody else can walk it for us,
> We have to walk it by ourselves.[1]

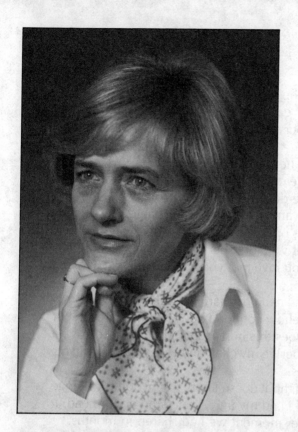

A portrait of me in 1978 when my first book, *For the Love of My Daughter,* was published.

Our family gathers for our Christmas celebration in 1979, just days before the fire. Sitting (from left to right): our son, Joel; Gene; myself; and our daughter, Jill. Standing: our son, Jack; Vicki, our daughter-in-law, and Jeff, our youngest son, with their baby, Jeremy; Grandma Ton; and Jill's husband, Bill McGregor.

One side of the Woodruff Place Baptist Church on the day of the fire, January 4, 1980. I climbed out of my office window on the opposite side of the church.

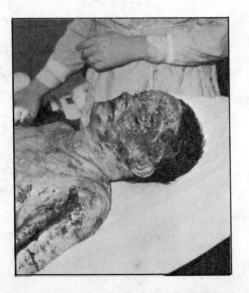

This picture is taken three weeks after the fire, during a dressing change. You can see the surgical cut on my arm from the escharotomy.

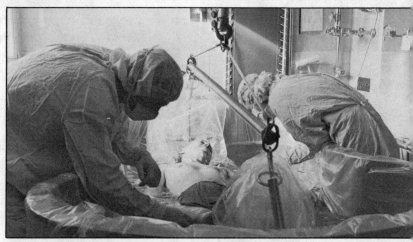

The Hubbard tank, in which I was suspended for debridement and to cleanse my wounds. The plastic sheet surrounding the tank is an additional guard against infection.

The hydrotherapy room, called "Tub City, Indiana" by burn patients who dreaded going there. One of the plinths against the back wall was attached to the lift device above the Hubbard tank to lower me into the water.

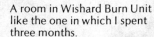

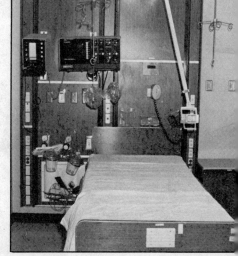

A room in Wishard Burn Unit like the one in which I spent three months.

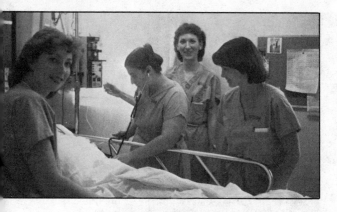

The "angels" of Wishard, nurses who valued my body when I felt it was too badly damaged to be of further use.

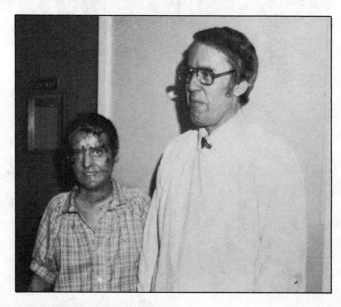

Gene and I as we leave the hospital on the day of my homecoming, March 14, 1980.

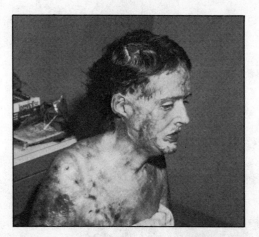

This picture is taken in the out-patient clinic the day I returned to the hospital because of a staph infection.

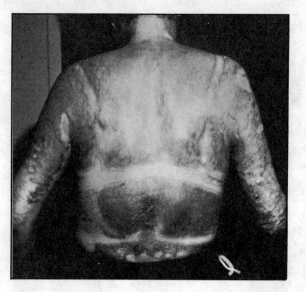

A back view taken the same day. The line of unburned skin was prote[cted] by my bra.

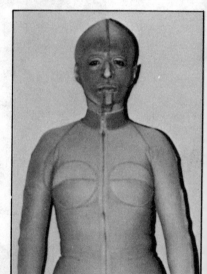

The Jobst garment I wore for almost a year.

My grandson, Jeremy, and I after he grew accustomed to grandmother's new image.

A picture taken one year after the fire; two reconstructive surgeries have already been performed.

The Mary Ellen Ton of today.

Gene and I in the den of our home in the fall of 1982.

11

Mirror, Mirror, on the Wall

"**I**'m getting worse, not better."

Those discouraging words spoken so often lately to Gene were like an epitaph. As the burns healed, the scar tissue began forming contractures. I sat and watched my fingers grow together, my left arm fasten itself to my trunk, and my neck thicken and grow stiff. I could neither force my arms down to my sides nor raise the left one more than a few inches above my waist. My eyelids pulled down exposing the red mucous lining, and each time I tried to turn my head the contractures pulled them down more. When I tried to do exercises to loosen my body and retard the contractures, it grew increasingly difficult and the tightness of my skin twisted and contorted my face into monsterlike grimaces.

Night after night I went to bed with one prayer on my lips. "Please, God, heal my face. Don't let it be scarred. Please, not my face. I can handle all the rest if you'll just let me have my face." But as my face refused to heal and infection broke down every hint of new skin forming, I knew in my heart that my face would be badly scarred.

This, more than anything else, haunted me day and night. I never thought much about scarring in the hospital. I don't know if that was because all my body's energies were focused on survival, or if I was blocking it out, or if it was simply naivete. Actually, I didn't consider the future much one way or the other.

Now that I was home and the days were turning into weeks, I was forced to take a look at what had really happened to me and the effects on the rest of my life. I didn't want to look ahead, refused to, and I didn't want to look behind either.

When I had hidden in the attic as a little girl, I would sometimes hear my mother calling me, "Mar-eee . . . Mary Ellen." But I had pretended not to hear because I wasn't ready to leave the security of my hiding place. Now, I heard Gene's voice calling, "Mary, Mary, we can make it. Let me in so I can touch you. Let me help you. We'll just take it one step at a time." But, I was too hurt, too afraid to come out.

"This is it," I told him. "This *is* how it's always going to be. Nothing can ever change it. You ought to leave. There's nothing here for you anymore. I can't be your wife; I can't even be a human being."

"You're still here. I love you. I love the person you were."

"But, don't you see, I'm not that person anymore. Mary Ellen Ton died on January 4."

To look back at the person I had been was far too painful. There was no resemblance between the lifeless, bleeding hulk I was now and the attractive, vibrant woman I had once been. Gene was a constant reminder of that other person. He became like a giant mirror reflecting back my ugliness. He tried so hard. I ached for his pain as well as my own. He wanted so much to help me, but everything he did hurt. When he reached out to touch my hand, I always remembered his words, "Ummmm, your hands feel sooo nice." When he most gingerly tried to put his arms around me, I recalled how urgently he had once needed me. All his endearing words of love, " . . . your smooth shoulders . . . soft lips," replayed in my mind like a broken record.

I had always needed Gene's reassurance that he loved me. In fact it had been impossible for him to give me enough love, enough attention, enough assurance, to ease my apprehension. For years before the accident we had traveled the same route over and over:

"But, honey, you know I love you," Gene would insist.

"Yes, but . . ."

"Have I ever given you any reason to doubt that?"

"No, but . . ."

"Then why can't you just accept it? I know you love me. I trust you. Why can't you trust me?"

"I don't know. I don't want to feel this way. It's awful! But I can't help how I feel."

Round and round we had gone, with me continually picking open this lone sore spot in our marriage and Gene trying to heal it once and for all.

I had always dreaded the days when his job called for him to travel away from home. Suddenly I found myself looking forward to those times. Not that I didn't miss him. I did, terribly. I wasn't accustomed to being shut in the house all alone, unable to get out to be with other people. But for a few brief days I experienced a sense of relief. When I zeroed in on this feeling, I realized it was because I didn't focus on my appearance when he was gone. But let him walk in the door, and I was overcome with my own grossness again. To be with him was to walk into a carnival's house of mirrors and see myself as distorted as I was.

The home-nursing care I received during this period of time was my only touch with the usual routine of daily life. Marinel's and Edie's coming was the bright spot in my day. Perhaps that exemplifies my desperation, since their coming brought physical pain as they helped me to shower and change the dressings. They spoke of newly admitted burn patients, reminding me I had already come a long way. Of course, the repeated flare-up of infections was frustrating and disappointing to them also, but they could remind me of each newly healed area. They were an eager audience whenever I told them of some minor achievement, like the day I figured out a way to open the washer and dryer.

Gene had put in a load of wash before he left for his office. He did this each morning, stripping my bed and running the sheets through the wash cycle. When he came home for dinner, he transferred them to the dryer. By night they were back on my bed ready for the whole procedure to be gone through the next morning. Even with this constant washing, the sheets soon bore the indelible outline of my body from all the blood, pus, and ointments.

I wanted so much to help him. More than that, I wanted to feel needed and useful. I had struggled for some time, trying to raise the lid on the washer. But it was no use. My hands simply would not cooperate and the pain became intolerable. Then I had an idea. By inserting the handle of a wooden spoon into the indentation intended for my fingers, using my palm to push down the bowl of the spoon, I was able to raise the lid enough to get my arm under it and open it the rest of the way. Now that I had conquered the washing machine, I tackled the dryer. Holding the rubber end of a spatula between my palms, I stuck the thin flat handle into the crack around the door; I used it as a pry to release the catch and the door popped open.

Next I had to extract the sheets from the washing machine. I scraped and scooped at them with the wooden spoon until I managed to get a piece over the agitator. I pinched it between my palms, dragging it out of the washer as I moved backwards. With the sheet on the open dryer door, I used the spoon again to push it into the dryer and shut the door.

The knob was more than I could handle. After one-half hour of thought and exertion, I could not turn the dryer on! I was frustrated and my hands hurt terribly, but I was strangely exhilarated. Completely exhausted by my endeavor, I sat in my chair waiting for the nurse to come.

When I told Edie what I had done, she was as excited as a mother over her baby's first step. She wrote in her nurse's note, "Mary Ellen did a load of wash. I am so proud of her." After she had gone and I stole a peek at her notes, I cried. I hadn't actually done a load of wash, but I was thrilled about what I had been able to do. When I read what she had written, I felt very much like a proud schoolgirl whose teacher had penciled in red, "Very well done!" across the top of her paper.

Marinel was also interested in my progress and in helping me avoid pain whenever possible. She soon realized the shower massage was giving more force to the water than my skin could endure. It felt like a million shots being injected simultaneously all over my body. The next day she came with a smaller shower head of her own and put it in place for me.

Agnes, another nurse, came when Marinel left to use one week of her vacation at a muscular dystrophy camp. She was older than Marinel and I wasn't sure I wanted a "stranger" coming in.

The first thing Agnes did was to purchase a very fine-toothed comb and go to work on some of the thick scabby areas of my head. I swallowed hard when she cut some of my brand-new hair off, but day by day, piece by piece, other burned places were debrided and prepared for healing. Then Agnes suggested that her husband, Joe, might come to fix up Marinel's and Gene's amateur job of hooking up the shower head, which left it squirting out all over the bathroom—so much so, that Agnes always got showered along with me. Joe came on a Sunday and repaired the fixture, taking a part home to rethread it, and returned again to install it. Soon I realized that Agnes was not a stranger, but another angel God had sent to help me.

One night Marinel appeared at the front door in a bed-sheet toga. She was on her way to a party. Imagine having a dressing change done by a beautiful young girl, wrapped in a white toga, with flowers in her upswept hair. She looked so pretty—and though I must admit to wondering what Gene thought as he looked at such a lovely creature after looking at me, it was a fun thing to share with her.

Each of these nurse's visits was a respite from my inner pain. I had reached the point where the physical pain was something to be endured and not to capitulate to. But it was my burning, searing inner pain that knew almost no relief. Something I did not understand was happening inside me. I was walking through an inner fire, and the emotional agony of it was more than any pain I had experienced on January 4. Again late in May I gave way to the unbearable rage I was feeling.

"I can't handle this," I told Gene. "It's too much. I wish I had died. I want only to die."

Perhaps Gene had had all he could bear, or perhaps he thought I needed a kick in the pants. I don't know, but his heated retort struck pay dirt. "You didn't die. You lived. You are alive whether you want to be or not. You can become bitter and ugly inside or you can fight back. It's up to you. I can't help you. I would take it on myself, if I could, but, I can't. You lived. You are alive. . . . It's up to you."

Later that same night I stood looking into the bathroom mirror as I clumsily attempted to brush my teeth. How could I live looking like this? Everything I had absorbed from the world around me told me I was a reject—a deviant, as one medical book stated. To be successful, indeed to be lovable, was synonymous with being beautiful.

But *beautiful* would never again be used as an adjective to describe my appearance. Indeed, not even *pretty*. Although my hair was beginning to grow, it still did not camouflage the bald grafted areas or my misshapen ears. The graft across my forehead was yellowish brown. I had not realized before how the color of my own skin varied. On my stomach the skin looked just right. On my face the same skin looked like what it was, a patch. I knew I would have patches under my eyes when surgery was done to release the scar tissue pulling them down. My face, aside from the grafts, was fiery red.

From observing other parts of my body that had been healed longer, I knew that the extreme redness would fade somewhat. But I also knew the telltale scars would always be there. I was filled with the same recurring panic as I faced the mirror and was confronted with the body I was imprisoned in forever. I was ugly. It hurt too much to live.

I was consistently receiving contradictory messages from other people. The strangers I encountered when Gene took me to the clinic were appalled. As I stepped onto an elevator, a heavy silence fell. Even clinic and hospital personnel hushed their friendly chatting to take furtive glances. Once when I stood talking to Ernie in the lobby, a receptionist openly stared the entire time. When I mentioned it to Ernie, he said, "That's her problem."

But it wasn't other people's problem, it was mine. I had no idea how to cope with being a freak. When I had lost the familiar facial characteristics I had grown so accustomed to, I lost my identity. I felt like a Jane Doe wandering in a vast no-man's-land. I wondered if this was, in some smaller way, like death when we lose our physical bodies. If it was, and if I really believed there was life beyond death, then I must somehow get in touch with the very essence of me. But how? How was I to grab hold of the reality of me in a world where I was stigmatized?

Friends were another story. At first I didn't want anyone to see me. Outside of my family and those strangers I walked past in the clinic, I saw no one. "I have to get used to myself first," I told Gene.

But one day in May when our good friends, Bill and Claribel Carson, called to check on us as they frequently did, Gene covered the mouthpiece of the phone with his hand. "They'd still like to come see you. They're not pushing . . . just letting you know."

I saw the hopefulness in his eyes and suddenly realized how lonely he was. My refusal to see people had cut him off from our friends, too. "It's all right; they can come if they want to."

Because there was a definite reluctance in my voice, Gene hesitated, "We're not pushing. Are you sure?"

"I'm sure," I said, even though my voice rang with uncertainty. "Just be sure you let them know how awful I look before they come."

Bill and Claribel came the very next evening. There was a flash of misgiving in their eyes, but there was something else, too. Acceptance. I recognized it immediately because it was the same look my family wore. It was a look that communicated: "Yes, I see how you have been disfigured, but it's OK with me."

After that visit, Bill Carson began to come once or twice a week to take me to clinic or physical therapy. The step up into his van was a monumental one for me. I stood in front of the open door and got on my mark. Then with a great deal of effort on my part and a push on the rear from Bill, I hoisted myself up and into the seat.

There was even a double message in a simple act like that. He would never have put his hands on that part of me before. It signaled my new estate, my differentness. At the same time, it told me how much these two people cared about the tragedy that had become so much a part of Gene's and my daily life.

On the way home, we often stopped at a nearby Baskin-Robbins 31 Flavors for a milk shake. Bill would go in to order while I waited in the van. The lines were clearly drawn as I sat there. Inside was a good friend who still believed in me; outside, walking past, were the gawking strangers.

I couldn't blame them for looking; I was a curious-looking creature. A part of me even understood. But another part of me shrank and shriveled under their eyes. Had it not been for the few, beautiful, good friends, who kept watering and nurturing the dead, brown seed lying dormant deep within me, there would have been only mold and decay. My family and friends believed in the possibility of new life.

One day, neither Bill nor Gene were available to take me to my physical therapy session. Gene mentioned that Ruth Wheeless, a lady I barely knew from our new church here in Indianapolis, had called to volunteer to help in any way she could. "I'd like to ask her to drive you tomorrow," he said. He was really asking, "Is it OK? Can you take another stranger?"

I realized Gene needed to get back into his work. Some degree of normalcy would be beneficial for both of us. I tried to sound enthusiastic, "Sure. That's great!" But I was afraid. It was scary to go out among strangers with a stranger. I needed someone familiar to give me support.

On the way to the hospital, I learned that Ruth had been a nurse. She felt free to talk openly about my appearance, enabling us to jump that hurdle in short order. Then the therapist invited her to come into the gym while I exercised. I was not at all sure I liked that idea, but Ruth smiled and chatted, completely at ease the whole time. Actually the other patients showed more curiosity than she did. On previous visits, I had chosen to go to the far back corner and tended to face the wall so I wouldn't feel on display. After that day, it was no longer so important what table I lay on.

Ruth became sort of a liaison between the church family and Gene and I. Every Wednesday, she would appear with dishes of prepared food. Those several meals each week took a big load from Gene's shoulders. I was as pleased by some act that relieved him as much as by what was done for me.

I felt so terribly guilty about the strain I had put him under. I kept apologizing for being unable to take care of the house, his clothes, and meals the way I always had. I suppose I had always felt I had to earn my way. I had felt a sense of pride that there were always clean socks in his drawer, a freshly ironed shirt in his closet, and a good dinner for two with candlelight ready and waiting. For the love of that man, I would have turned myself inside out. My highest ambition had been to be his wife and a good one, whatever that might take.

My inability to fill any of those important roles added to my feelings of uselessness and despair. When I walked into the utility room on a Sunday morning and saw him fumbling to iron his own shirt, I ached for him and for me. I couldn't be his attractive hostess anymore. I couldn't fill his bed. I couldn't even iron his shirt. Everything that held meaning for me had burned up in the fire along with my body.

All the voices that had whispered to me through the years, taunting me with tales of my own worthlessness, seemed to scream in chorus: "You never were good enough for him, not from the very beginning. His own mother tried to tell you. You never went to college—never did anything well, except get pregnant. Now look at you. You can't even iron a shirt, and you're ugly . . . ugly . . . ugly. . . ."

Words spoken to me years before by a well-intentioned church member rang so loudly in my mind I wanted to cover my ears to keep my head from reverberating. One day she had confided to me. "I always felt so sorry for your husband." She had meant it as a compliment, intending to imply she had changed her opinion that I was not an asset to Gene once she had come to know me. Still, I had felt discovered.

I wondered how many people felt sorry for Gene now. I couldn't blame them. No man deserved to be stuck for life with a wife who looked as I now looked. I had sat around more than one table enjoying a cup of coffee while listening to Gene's friends lament that so-and-so's wife was no asset to him. More often than not, it was the woman's appearance being appraised and consequently devalued. On what scale would I be evaluated now? I wondered. I ached for a way to set Gene free.

If only we could go back! If we could go back to that morning of the fire and I could have stayed at home; if only we could go back to Christmas; if only we could go back to 1977 and our church in Evansville. We had been happy there. The kids had grown up, only Joe was still at home. We had experienced a new kind of freedom. Gene was content in his role as pastor and so proud of some of the church's accomplishments. I had grown by leaps and bounds and felt so happy to discover parts of myself I hadn't known. My first book was published and I had danced with God in my kitchen. It didn't matter that I had never taken a creative writing course, never been to college. I felt my uniqueness as a child of God that day as I never had before. Now I longed to move backwards. The present was unbearable and the future hopeless.

Our move to Indianapolis had surely been an anathema, I thought. Gene had gone through his personal time of inner crisis, a struggle that carried us apart until there had been vast gray and black spaces between us. We had still been trying to move some pieces of the furniture of our lives into those empty spaces when the fire had struck. Little wonder Gene had cried out to the hospital walls, "She can't die; she can't die. She doesn't know I love her." Now that I was burned and scarred beyond recognition, I knew that neither Gene nor any other man could ever really love me. If we could be so alienated when I was at my best—pretty and vibrant and growing—how could he possibly love the wasted, ugly creature I had been turned into?

12

I Pack My Grandfather's Trunk

Ever since I can remember I have enjoyed a perennial case of spring fever, evidenced by the need to get out-of-doors and to daily inspect each bush, tree, and nose-peeking green thing. When the children were small, I infected them with this fever and together we listed "first symptoms" on the bulletin board. "Pussy willow . . . Jill; green nose of a tulip . . . Jack; robin . . . Joey; coatless kid . . . dad; green tree bud . . . Jeff; lilac buds . . . mom." It is a fever for which the numerous passing seasons provide no immunization.

But those early spring days of 1980 had been different. Though the sun had begun to warm the earth and the gentle rains had washed away the last traces of winter, I sat dormant, covered with the mold of grief and slowly beginning to decay. The forsythia must have bloomed; the robins surely built their nests again; spring must have come that year. But, as I sat slumped in my chair in the den or wearily trudged through the house, mother nature's dressing change went unnoticed.

Who can describe the miracle at work deep within the core of a bulb? To dig it up and dissect it in a vain attempt to discover this secret is to risk the bulb's very life. Like the bulb, my soul lay buried and dormant during this winter of my life. But the mystery was at work deep within.

It reminded me of the silly little game played at birthday

parties when I was a child called I Packed My Grandfather's Trunk. The leader would begin, "I packed my grandfather's trunk and in it I put his long red flannel nightshirt." The next person continued, "I packed my grandfather's trunk and in it I put his long red flannel nightshirt . . . and his blue and yellow striped suspenders." And so the game went on, with the next person listing each article packed and adding one more item. It was obvious, though never mentioned, that grandfather was going on a long trip and he must be well prepared for any and all emergencies.

Perhaps I had played that game all through childhood and on into my adult years, packing into my trunk each life experience: every learning and growth, each decision, insight, and gift. Perhaps, unknown to me, God had joined in the game with me, helping me to pack everything I would need for my present journey out of the fire.

Once during this time I had tried to describe to a friend how I felt. "I loved God and trusted him and gave him the best that I knew and he betrayed me," I had told her. "He left me hanging on a window ledge screaming for help."

My friend had sadly shaken her head, and I had known she felt sorry for me. Not so much because I had been badly burned, but because my faith had not been strong enough to carry me through.

That's where she was wrong! I have never been a pacifist in my relationship to God. Our at-one-ment has been hammered out blow by blow. After I first met him in my teenage years, there were times when I had doubted his reality, questioned his existence and my own experience with him. But, no more! Packed in the trunk of my experience was a strong and deep belief in God. I never questioned he was with me through the fire; I simply did not understand the role he played in it. I had much to learn.

I had spent a lot of time looking through photo albums during those early spring days of 1980. It was a heartbreaking experience to see myself as I had been, and yet there was a deep need in me to hang onto that person, too. The visible image had a hypnotic effect. When I looked at my smiling, pretty, blemish-free face, my smooth arms and hands, the rings on my fingers, and my frosted blonde hair, I could almost *be* that woman again in my mind. Gene had been willing to bring my picture to the hospital and hang it on my bulletin board, but now he was bewildered by my need to haunt the present with the past.

"Put the pictures away, Mary," he had urged. "Don't torture yourself this way." Whenever he found pictures laying out, he carefully picked them up and put them away in a new place.

One day, as I sat weeping and grieving over the pictures, I suddenly remembered something my mother had done. After my father died she had all but covered the walls of her bedroom with his photographs, some as old as World War I when he had served as a soldier. I had realized that it was her way of hanging on to him so a part of her life wouldn't die with him. But as the months had turned into years, it became a little morbid and frightening. "How can she ever pick up the pieces of her life and move on if she lives back there?" I had worried to Gene.

It struck me that I was doing exactly the same thing, using my pictures to hang on to someone who was dead. The lady in those pictures had died in a fire. I had to let her go. Maybe in some deep inner part of me I had known this all along.

Slowly, methodically, crying aloud like a small child, I tore every picture into pieces: pictures of Gene and me at seventeen and fourteen, when we had first started dating; our wedding pictures; pictures of a young woman with a baby and then two, three, and four little children. Finally there was the twenty-fifth anniversary photo Gene had brought to the hospital and a lovely portrait Gene had had finished after my first book was published. My life history filled half of a large grocery bag, fragments of a woman who had been and was no more.

An image of myself based on the way I used to look,

and a self-esteem and confidence grounded on my appearance, was no longer useful to me. My womanliness and sexuality seemed to be bound to this lost image. Before I completely discarded this woman, I knew I needed to work hard to coax these parts of my personality to live in my new, strange body. Without them I had come to think of myself as an "it."

An immeasurable part of my self-concept had been acquired through the eyes of other persons—how they saw me, felt about me, liked me. It had been made quite obvious to me that the concept others had of me had been drastically changed. Only a few members of my own family and two or three close friends had any idea how to relate to me at all, much less intimately. Even little Jeremy, my grandson, didn't know me and refused any overtures I tried to make.

Ever since he had first visited me in the hospital we knew he was afraid of the peculiar-looking creature everyone referred to as "grandma." He watched me with a great deal of curiosity, but always from a safe distance. I would talk to him as he sat playing on the floor in the den.

Now when I spoke to him, Jeremy would look up, stare intently back at me, but make no move to respond. The separation hurt me, but we all felt it was best to let him take his own time in adjusting to the new me.

One day he had wandered into the living room and was peeking out the little window in the front door. He delighted in this because most windows were up too high for a little guy to see out. I was taking one of my walks around the house and we saw each other at the same time. He stood absolutely still, confused and frightened to find himself suddenly alone with me.

I had the good sense to stop in my tracks and not take another step toward him. When he realized I wasn't going to advance on him, he turned tail and scooted to the safety of the kitchen and his mother. It was a sickening feeling to frighten a little child, even though I knew how I must look to him.

Then it had happened. Weeks later, on a day like so many other days, Jeremy was sitting on the floor wrestling with Gene. I was talking to him and smiling at the two of them when suddenly Jeremy got up, walked over to where I was sitting, and ever so gently laid his little face in my lap and hugged my knees.

My son, Jeff, started to say something to him because he knew how tender my upper legs were, but I quickly shook my head at him. Of course, it hurt. But my heart was dancing and never noticed. I laid my hand on Jeremy's head, feeling his soft blond curls as tears ran down my cheeks. A little boy and his grandmother had just unpacked a trunk together.

As May turned into June, I discovered many things packed in the trunk, things as small as a brief phrase from a song tickling at the back of my mind.

"Because he lives, I can face tomorrow. . . . Because he lives, I can face tomorrow! . . ." Over and over and over again, that brief phrase ran through my mind. I had first heard the song at Crooked Creek Baptist Church. It must have been one of that congregation's favorites. Even when a group gathered informally around a piano, it was sung with gusto. That one line was all I could remember as it haunted my mind for days.

Finally, because it would not let me go, I called the pastor's wife, Virginia Sutton, and asked her to send me the words. She not only mailed the words to me but the printed music as well. Now, at last, I could read the whole song.

> Because he lives, I can face tomorrow.
> Because he lives, all fear is gone.
> Because I know . . . I know he holds my
>   future
> Life is worth the living
> Just because he lives.[1]

I didn't know exactly how the tune went; I never had

learned to read notes. It really didn't matter anyway because my vocal cords had been damaged by the toxins in the heat and smoke, and I couldn't sing. So I croaked out the words in my unique froglike style as I made the circle around our house carrying the purses that the physical therapist had suggested would help to pull my arms down into a more natural position at my sides. Maybe at first I was whistling in the dark. All fear was certainly not gone. I was scared, scared of the future I saw ahead of me, scared I didn't have the guts it would take to face tomorrow. Even so, from past experiences, I believed that God would somehow move to meet my needs. Deep inside I waited expectantly for what might happen.

Before long, I found myself wanting to know how the song really sounded. I sent the music to my sister-in-law, Gloria, who had a lovely voice, asking her to please record it for me. She did better than that. She had a record of the entire cantata and made a tape for me.

Several weeks passed before I actually listened to the tape. I had been pretty depressed and wasn't in the mood to even try to sing it. One day in early June I stretched out on one of the twin beds in the guest room and turned on the recorder. As usual when God takes us by surprise, I was not prepared for what followed.

As I lay there listening, I had the urge to turn the volume up louder and louder until the music beat at me. For a few minutes, it seemed to form a sound barrier, blocking out everything else. There was no pain. There was no itching. There was only the swelling of the beautiful music and the words of faith being sung. Then there occurred one of those rare and awesome experiences. Suddenly it seemed as though I (the I that is really me) left that burned-up body lying on the bed and was enveloped by the presence of God's spirit. I felt a great sense of relief and, if you can understand this, I felt clean.

You might think that I would shoot all the questions I had broiling inside me at God, once I recognized his presence. But for those few holy moments, none of those questions entered my mind. There seemed to be no need to ask them. For the time nothing mattered except that God *was* and I *was*. I began to have a somewhat faint awareness of what it might mean to walk through the fire and not be burned. "When you pass through the waters I will be with you; and through the rivers, they shall not overwhelm you; when you walk through fire you shall not be burned, and the flame shall not consume you" (Isa. 43:2, RSV).

If ever there was a song to walk through fire by, "Because He Lives" became it for me. I croaked it in the shower as blood from open wounds ran into the tub. I hummed it while rubbing raw areas with peroxide and while walking around the backyard, my purses pulling at the stiffened joints and muscles in my arms. Even when the words weren't coming out of my mouth, they were crooning around in my head. But most of all, I tried to claim them as my own each time I looked into the mirror and was startled by the reflection staring back at me.

There was no great theological revelation in those moments. I learned no new truth about Christian faith. I simply felt the presence of God in a way that for me was quite different than normal.

I had had a similar experience once before. It was in 1956, when I was twenty-three years old. Gene and I were living in married students' housing on the Northern Baptist Theological Seminary campus in Chicago. I had just hauled Jill who was one and a bag of clothes down four flights of stairs to the laundry room and back up to our apartment, when the pain came suddenly as I was unlocking the apartment door. I put the baby on the floor and quickly sat down to catch my breath. But it would not be caught! The room, the children, floated in front of me. I found myself doubled up in a ball on the couch, clutching my stomach, observing everything around me through a bubble of pain.

Then, as abruptly as it had begun, it had stopped. As the day passed, I was certain it could not have been nearly as bad as I had imagined at the time. And then it struck again with fierce intensity.

We had no insurance, no money for doctor's bills, so I put off calling that day and the next. But the pain was relentless and came with increasing frequency, even after I had given in and visited my doctor who had found nothing wrong.

When periodic hemorrhaging began to occur, I jumped at a neighbor's suggestion to call her gynecologist.

The doctor's probing had seemed to cause everything inside me to break loose. The pain was excruciating. It knocked the wind out of me, preventing even the simplest answer to any of his questions.

He explained that he was certain I had a tubal pregnancy and that I must go directly to the hospital for immediate surgery.

Only a few hours later, before Gene or anyone else had arrived at the hospital, I found myself swathed in stiff sheets from head to toe, parked on a gurney outside the operating room door. Somewhere down the corridor behind my head, nurses spoke in hushed voices. Strange sounds seemed to bounce at me from every direction. Never before had I felt so completely alone.

I had begun to think I might die without ever seeing Gene or my babies again. I could feel the fear rising up in me like something alive and growing, filling me so full I knew it was going to come screaming out my mouth.

Then, just at the very peak of my panic . . . God was there. I saw nothing, heard nothing, but I knew. It was the same feeling you have when you're sitting in a room with your back to the door and you know someone has entered the room. I had never felt his presence this way before. *O God,* I thought, *all that stuff I said I believed . . . it's really true. You are for real. You really are.*

The panic subsided as quickly as it had come, the choking fear left me, and in its place was a sense of trust. I was still afraid. I still didn't want to die. But I felt God's plan had been good for me in life and would be good for me in death. The last thing I remember thinking as I started gasping for the anesthetic was *I am OK now. Thanks.*

Sometime between losing consciousness on the operating table and dawn, I woke up in the darkness of my own room. Still feeling enveloped by the wonder-filled experience, I reached out my hand as though to clasp one extended to me. In reality, of course, it closed on air. But in another sense far beyond reality, it held something very precious. For I held in my hand, never to let go again, the certain awareness that God is. I *knew* the one whom I had only believed in before.

Now, twenty-five years later, I still remember that night and the assurance I felt. It was not the beginning of my relationship with God, nor the sum total. But it was not unlike a wedding. Preceded by courtship, followed by years of living and growing together, the wedding itself becomes a special moment in time, an event to change the course of a life. Something had happened between God and me in the midst of that past experience. Some unspoken commitments had been made, some unseen bonds established to start me on a new adventure.

As the events that were part of that long-ago experience replayed in my mind, I began to make comparisons to this new experience of God's presence. Both had occurred at a point when I seemed to run out of coping resources, when I was alone, frightened, and completely vulnerable. Both had given me the simple assurance that God was a reality and that he was there, aware of all that was happening to me. Both had touched a part of me that was not physical, a part that remained basically the same despite pain, death, and disfigurement.

I realized this was the part of me, the only part of me, salvageable from the fire. I wondered if I could hold onto that sense of trust and assurance in the long months ahead. It would have to be affirmed and reaffirmed and affirmed yet again.

Because he lives, I can face tomorrow
Because he lives, all fear is gone.
Because I know . . . I know he holds my
   future
Life is worth the living
Just because he lives.

My trunk was full and running over.

13

A Funny Thing Happened On My Way to Life

"I think you should get one. After all you've been through you should have anything, anything at all that might make you happy." My daughter-in-law, Vicki, fairly exploded the words.

We had been talking about buying a puppy as Gene cleared the lunch dishes away from the kitchen table. For several weeks I had alternated between listing all the reasons why I should get a dog and all the reasons why it wasn't such a hot idea. Vicki's words erupted with surprising suddenness, because she had said little about the accident. The intense feeling in her voice communicated to me the depth of her caring.

The first normal decision I made on my own behalf in over five months was to dial a number out of the want ads advertising miniature schnauzer pups for sale. Gene had been waiting for me to take the initiative. As soon as he came home from work and I told him what I had done, he called and made arrangements to pick up a puppy. And I had interpreted his hesitation as reluctance!

After dinner that evening in the middle of June, Muffet came to live with me. I had made a quick decision to ride along with Gene when he drove over to pick her up. It was a lengthy drive across the city; my first venture out other than visits to the clinic. For the first time that year, I saw that spring had come. It was everywhere. Late tulips and clumps of yellow daffodils bordered the paths to homes along the way. The trees, already fully leafed but still bearing that fresh, new green color, looked as though they were trying to touch fingertips across the streets. I could scarcely believe my eyes. Like magic, mother nature had waved her wand and turned winter into spring. To me, it seemed to have happened overnight.

Gene parked the car a few houses away from the number we were looking for. I didn't want any curious eyes peering out of windows at me. When he came back out to the car and placed the warm, wiggly bit of fur in my lap, I knew something important had happened. Little Miss Muffet, wrapped in a scrap of brown blanket from her box-home, nestled down into my lap, so little she didn't hurt a bit. I stroked her with my stubby, clumsy hand. She didn't mind that they didn't look normal. Muffie, as we immediately nicknamed her, began at once to cover them with eager puppy kisses. I couldn't help but smile as I wondered what my nurses would think about that!

On the drive home, Gene told me the owner of the male and female dogs was an invalid. When Gene had shared with him my anxiety over being unable to care for the pup, he had shown Gene his own hands, which were crippled. "She can do it, if I can," he had affirmed. Earlier that same day he had sold another puppy to a terminal cancer patient. It seems I was not alone in reaching out to a small animal for comfort.

Muffie became more than just a solace to me. She was companionship during long, lonely hours. I had been used to working each day and being involved with many different people. Now the hours alone at home were heavy and trudged by slowly. Gene was often gone in the evening and took frequent trips out of town. Muffie filled the empty spaces. No matter how much it hurt to bend and stoop and lift, she needed care. Scooping her out of her box, taking her in and out to housebreak her, handling her food and water dishes made me do things in spite of the pain. With every passing week my body began to respond. The bending became easier, my hands less awkward. And, most amazing of all, Muffie made me laugh, even though I thought I would never see anything funny again. I began to giggle at her antics and feel needed again.

The doctor had suggested a drug to ease my extreme depression. But instead, a furry, little black puppy became my antidepressant. I will never forget the day, later that summer, when Muffie and I were out in the backyard and got caught in a sudden summer shower. It wasn't until I was in the shelter of the screened-in porch that I suddenly realized I had run. I had actually run across the yard and onto the porch! I laughed for the sheer delight of it.

Little Miss Muffet will never look like a proper schnauzer. When the time came for her to have her ears cropped so they would stand erect like a well-groomed dog of her breed, I didn't have the heart to do it. My own badly burned ears were still covered with open, seeping places and were unbearably tender just to touch. I couldn't bring myself to have her little ears cut. So, Muffie's ears flop, which isn't proper. But, then, I don't look proper myself.

On a bright and sunny day late in June, I went out into the garage, looking for an old Frisbee that Gretchen, my son Joe's dog, had played with as a toy. There was something on a shelf above my head just out of reach. Maybe that was it. I couldn't see what it was from where I was standing.

I strained to get my right arm up over my head and began to clumsily scoop at the object. I could see now it wasn't the Frisbee, but, with my curiosity aroused, I was still determined to bring it down. Finally it fell. I caught it in my arms, clutching it to my chest.

The smell sent me reeling backwards. I caught my balance by backing into the front end of the car, at the same time dropping the objects I had worked so hard to get.

The purse and gloves lying on the concrete floor at my feet were charred and still reeking of smoke. The sight and smell of them sent me whirling back in time to that room in Woodruff Place Baptist Church.

The shock of suddenly coming upon the purse and gloves I had carried to work that day knocked the breath out of me. I stooped to pick them up. "No . . . oh, no . . ." I cried. "It's over; it's over. I'm all right." But the instant replay had already started. No matter how tightly I shut my eyes, I saw it all again: the smoke, black and ominous, swirling in the hall; the woman slumped on the floor and then hanging onto the window ledge.

All the pictures I had tried to shut out of my mind danced in front of the windows of my soul. And the pictures were not without sound effects. I could hear the woman screaming, "Help, help, somebody help me." And then she called her God with the uncluttered words used by desperate people, "Oh, God . . . oh, my God . . . God . . . God."

Huge sobs racked my body as I bent to retrieve the purse and gloves. I held them close to me and rocked back and forth. *Poor things,* I thought, *they're just like me, burned stiff, scorched, and scarred, no longer fit for anything but the trash can.*

Ceremoniously, I lifted the lid off the garbage can, standing just inside the door of the garage, and dropped the articles one at a time into the dark recesses of the plastic liner. There was so much I had to part with: pictures, remnants from the fire, and large pieces of myself. Somehow I knew, as I heard each article hit the bottom of the can—a soft pat with each glove, a loud thump from the purse—a part of myself was going, too. As I turned my back on the can and walked across the garage and into the kitchen, I took my first faltering steps out of the fire.

I never really thought about it, but perhaps that June was a little like walking in on the middle of a movie. I couldn't really understand what was happening to me or conceive how it might all end without seeing the beginning. Maybe because the shock of the fire was so great, I cannot consciously remember how I managed to climb out the small window. I needed to go back in my mind and think myself out of that room. I don't pretend to understand how the mind works. I only know my journey back into that room seemed to allow me to walk out of it.

Another strange incident happened shortly after that. My hands were becoming more functional. With each new day, I found I could accomplish a few more minor tasks around the house. One day I decided I would tidy up the den. Because I usually stayed in there, it had become cluttered with various odds and ends. Gene's desk was a particular mess with home-care instructions from the hospital, splints, used envelopes, letters, cards, hair clips, tubes of ointment and pencils, pens, and paper clips strewn all over it. As I sorted through the accumulation, I found a letter that had been incorrectly addressed and returned to us. I opened it to discover a Christmas card. Further down in the pile was one of our own unsent Christmas cards, never put away.

I ignored the peculiar feelings that began to gnaw at my stomach. To divert my thoughts, I went to the stereo and struggled to remove the dust protector. There were some records resting on the turntable. When I gingerly turned the table so I could see the record titles, the gnawing feeling took one huge bite. The top one was Jackie Gleason's *Merry Christmas* album.

I walked around the house with the numbness of having been whirled backwards in time. It was an eerie feeling, coming upon remnants of Christmas in the month of June. How spooky! It was like coming into a house where someone had died and picking up after them.

One final incident that happened during June took me back to a time before the fire—and helped to move me forward into the future. Some of the women from Gene's former church in Lebanon embroidered a wall hanging for me. It was a picture of a large sunflower growing out of a Campbell's tomato soup can, which had been custom framed by one of the laymen. On it were carefully stitched words—Bloom Where You Are Planted Now, a well-known

Christian slogan and the title of a speech I had given to the women's club a little over a year ago.

April of '79 had been a bad time for me to think about "blooming." Gene and I had been working hard to fit the pieces of our relationship back together. The shape of ourselves had changed as we began our journey through mid-life, so the process of examining the pieces, twisting and turning them, trying to make them fall into place, was frustrating. The possibility that we might not fit back together perfectly was something I had refused to accept.

I am an incorrigible dreamer. I dreamed of the beautiful princess who married her handsome prince and lived happily ever after in the perfect castle-home with their perfect children. I suppose when my sand castle was washed away as Jill rebelled against the perfect image I had set up for her, I had clung all the more tenaciously to what was left of the beautiful princess, who although she might not have proven to be the perfect mother, was still the perfect wife for the prince.

But then the prince had problems. I confess I was afraid when the man I married, who always knew just what to do and when to do it, didn't. He was the strong one, the dependable one, the one who had it all together, the one the kids and I believed could hold all of us up, and himself, too. I didn't want him to have any problems. I didn't want him to have any doubts. I didn't want him to be afraid. It was all right for me; it was all right for the children; but it was not all right for Gene.

When one night as we lay side by side in our bed he had confessed, "Sometimes I feel like a scared little boy. I feel like my whole world is crumbling," I didn't want to hear. My theme song for over twenty-five years of marriage had been, "I am weak, but Gene is strong." In no way was I prepared to have this role reversed. When Gene had withdrawn to spend more and more time by himself to search for answers to the questions that burned in his soul, I had thought only of my own exclusion. When he had acted in strange and unfamiliar ways, I panicked. When in response to my incessant barrage of probing questions, he had admitted it was for him a time of doubting his job, his calling, his abilities, and himself, my lines of understanding had been jammed with my own disillusionment.

Had that been the extent of it, I probably would have hung on to at least a part of my dream; but when at last he had told me he doubted his love for me, I had felt the dream shatter. I had done everything wrong. I ranted, raved, argued, cajoled, begged, and pleaded—and at last resorted to throwing stones. I had pelted this beautiful man, who had stood by me through the crisis between Jill and me with love and encouragement, with accusing questions. I had the strength to hurl large rocks: "What would your former congregations think of you now? What about all your crisis counseling? What did all your sermons mean if they can't help you? Were they just empty words?"

But I had not had the strength to offer him gentleness, patience, or understanding, much less a little acceptance.

I had done a lot of reading during that time. The most helpful book was *Men in Mid-Life Crisis* by Jim Conway.[1] It had helped me to identify what was in all likelihood happening to Gene at that point in his life and as a result to me. I had also developed a little compassion for friends who no doubt were experiencing the same crisis, though it went unnamed. I had gained some insights into the mysterious nature of men, and, I hoped, some understanding of the problem. But, at that time, I held no understanding for Gene. There had been times when I had reached out, times when my mouth said the right things, but in the end I flunked the course.

We had come into the new year of 1979 with the storm behind us, but had found our lives cluttered by the debris left in the wake.

Gene is a person who can easily leave things behind and move on. I, on the other hand, cling tenaciously to the past, the good and the bad of it. There is something in me that holds onto hurts. I preferred not to look at that specter, but inside I had known it was on my agenda for growth.

Gene had been able to see the past year or two as a part of the process of growth, while I had nurtured the hurt, viewed his doubts as facts, and refused to be assured of his continuing love for me. His "I'm not even certain I love you," taken out of context had become, "I don't love you."

While Gene had been trying in every way imaginable to show me his love, I had been unable or unwilling to accept his affirmations.

In that context I had prepared my talk for the April women's meeting. Now, in the middle of another crisis, the words were echoed back to me on a wall hanging. Bloom Where You Are Planted. I went looking for my notes from that meeting. What I read amazed me.

BLOOM WHERE YOU ARE PLANTED

There are times in my life when the phrase I want to hear least of all is: Bloom where you are planted now!

The reason is quite simple: to bloom requires growing, and growth for me has always been painful. In fact, I can readily identify with the little seed in this children's story. I think you will discover a bit of yourself in it as well.

Once upon a time, two little grains of wheat grew side by side. They were both born and raised on the same "head," that is, the part of the wheat stalk that contains the seed.

The two grains were close friends. They had grown up together. Outwardly you might say they were identical twins. Yet there was a world of difference between them.

One was bright, gay, and unselfish. The other was vain, proud, and self-centered, thinking that every field mouse and meadowlark that came by looked only at it.

The two seeds were harvested and put in a tall grain elevator. One very cold day the selfish grain asked the other, "What do you think will happen to me now?"

The other grain patiently replied, "Let's listen to the seeds lying outside. Maybe they can tell us."

From the seeds nearest the outside they learned that they would be planted: placed in the ground and covered up with dirt. Later their beautiful brown, shiny coats would be split wide open by sprouts from inside themselves.

The selfish seed began to weep. "How horrible! How perfectly horrible. We've never done anything to deserve it. And do you realize that I was probably the loveliest seed on our entire stalk? Or, in the whole field, for that matter. . . . I won't sprout. I won't, I tell you!"

"They say that if you don't sprout, you die and rot and nobody remembers you. I'd think twice if I were you," said the other, trying to talk sense into its brother's head.

"I'll take my chances," it replied. "At least I know what I'm like now, and that's better than changing."

Soon afterward all the millions of wheat seeds in the elevator were loaded into large wagons, and then were dumped into a seed-planting machine. The selfish grain shrieked with horror, protesting all the while that it wouldn't go.

As fate would have it, the two grains fell into the ground side by side and no sooner landed than a layer of moist black dirt fell on top of them. About the third day they both awoke with splitting headaches. My, how they hurt!

Actually their pain was quite natural. You might call them growing pains they were so natural, pains that somehow come to us all in the process of growing up.

From what they had overheard back in the elevator, they both realized that they were about to sprout.

The selfish seed cried angrily, "I won't sprout, I tell you!"

The unselfish seed replied, "Frankly, I'm not crazy about the idea myself, but it's the only way I'll ever see the sun, the trees, the lovely blue sky, or the meadowlarks again. And you don't really die. You know that. You simply change form and live far more wonderfully than before. It's just being willing to give yourself up that's the hard part."

But the other was stubborn. "I'm not committing suicide. Go ahead if you want to."

"Well, here goes. Ouch! My head! Oh-o-o-o-o-o-o-o-o-o-o-o-oh! My beautiful coat is splitting. There now, it's over. I'll never be the same again. Please come. It's my last chance to talk with you."

But the selfish seed said no.

The freshly sprouted seed sent a lovely green shoot upward through the moist soil and peeked out at the loveliest, brightest blue sky it had ever seen. It drew on its remaining strength to send a tender root to draw up more food and water. Above, as its head shot higher, it saw thousands of other wheat plants, pastel green in color, thrusting their way upward toward the life-giving sun. Meadowlarks shot past full of cheerful song.

Under the dark soil lay the poor little selfish seed, its body now dead and decaying.[2]

After sharing this story with the women, I had gone on to quote from John Powell's book, *The Secret of Staying in Love*:[3]

"Life is a death-resurrection cycle. In every moment there is a death, a leaving what has been, and a birth, a stepping into what is and will be. We must leave things behind."

Bob Dylan said the same thing in other words, "He who is not busy being born, is busy dying."[4]

I have been having a particularly hard time dealing with the theme given me for tonight. I sat down several times in the last few weeks to put something together, only to give up on it. And I knew why! You remember I told you I could really identify with one of the seeds in the story? Well, at this point in my life I find myself shouting for all I'm worth, "I won't sprout. I won't grow. I won't, I tell you."

It only seems right to talk to persons about growing when your own bud is in full blossom. Not when you feel like you're rotting away under a layer of dirt. That's why I was having such a difficult time putting this talk together.

But then one of God's mini-miracles happened. Last night, as I was looking through a concordance for a particular scripture verse

I wanted to use, I stumbled onto a different one and once again the Bible became for me the "living Word of God."

Isaiah 43:18 in the Good News Bible begins, "But the Lord says." I would like to take the liberty of changing that just a bit to read, "But the Lord said to Mary Ellen, 'Do not cling to events of the past or dwell on what happened long ago. Watch for the new thing I am going to do. It is happening already—you can see it now! I will make a road through the wilderness and give you streams of water there.' "[5]

Isn't that the moral of the story of the two seeds? Forget the past and what has been. Look for the new thing God is doing in your life. Isn't that what Powell and Dylan are talking about? Leave what has been and step into what is and will be. And isn't that what Jesus was talking about when he said, "Be born again"?

I believe in God's continuing work in my life, even now when I really feel buried. I believe I have within me the possibility to bloom again and again and again. I believe now just as firmly as I did over a year ago when I blossomed on my stalk and reached for the sky.

I don't know where you are in the cycle of growth. Perhaps tonight you are "on your stalk"—blooming. You are feeling great and celebrating the uniqueness of being you.

Or, having experienced the miracle of new life in the growth process for yourself, you are encouraging someone else—urging them toward life.

Or, you may be harvested in some secure

resting place, experiencing a time of peace
and quiet in your life.

Perhaps on the other hand, like me, this
may be a time of terrifying change and
growth. Maybe a death, a move, loss of a
job, sickness, the kids leaving home, divorce, retirement, or a heartbreaking disappointment in a child or a husband, has
torn you up by the roots.

Wherever you find yourself on this never-
ending cycle, can you hear God's words
coming to you tonight? Grow. Bloom.
Bloom where you are planted now.

When you look at a seed, there is no
doubt that new life is hidden inside. Claim
the promise of new life inside yourself. New
life always demands giving up the old.

To bloom requires the dark night of being
planted—the pain of growth.

The words leaped off the printed page, capered around
the room, waved their magic wand, and transformed me a
second time into the Little Seed. I heard myself speaking all
its lines: "I've never done anything to deserve this; I was
such a lovely seed; I won't sprout; I won't, I tell you; I don't
want to change."

I read my own words of affirmation. "I believe in God's
continuing work in my life and I believe I have within me the
possibility to bloom again."

I slid off the edge of the bed and knelt beside it, crying
again like a small child. But these tears were different somehow. They were not tears of anger or frustration, not tears of
despair or fear, they were not tears of pain. I had cried all
those tears before. These were tears of healing. They began
to extinguish the fire that still burned within me.

My prayer began where it had left off on January 4:
"Oh, God . . . Oh, my God . . . God." Only this time there

was no terror in the words. I laughed as I cried and told him, "I do believe that, I really do. I believed it then and I believe it now. It's been there all the time, hasn't it, packed in my trunk, buried under a bunch of junk."

My beautiful brown, shiny coat had been split wide open by a tragic fire. But the miracle was within.

Once I read that there are "born again" Christians and Christians who are born again and again. Surely I am one of those who is born again and again and again. The labor had been long and arduous, hazardous and painful, but then, God never has done a cesarean section. Prognosis: the newborn survived the birth process and she will LIVE.

14

Sifting through the Ashes

Had anyone bothered to ask me if I was an investor in The Great Insurance Company in the sky, I would certainly have denied it. But my gut-level reactions to my tragic accident had indicated I was a stockholder in good standing. My head would not have given assent to the idea that God promised to protect me from all harm—deliver me from all evil—if I only believed. But my inner rage at God had spoken out that theology, loud and clear. I had felt betrayed, as though God had failed to live up to some unwritten contract.

My prayers had always consisted of the terms of the contract: "God, bless my family tonight. Give my kids a safe trip home, Lord. Don't let anything happen to Gene; I couldn't bear it. Father, bless my marriage, safeguard it. Heal. . . . Protect. . . . Guide. . . . Give me. . . ." In return for the investment of my life, I had expected full coverage.

During those long, hot summer days of 1980, I continued to sing my theme song, "Because He Lives." But, many times, I sang it with tears streaming down my cheeks, my voice catching and breaking over the words. There were dark places in my valley that no one, not even Gene, could walk with me. I still affirmed, though sometimes faintly, the belief that resurrection would follow my death by fire. But I was living on Saturday. Sunday morning, resurrection day, had not yet dawned.

Sometimes I felt as though I was riding a giant roller coaster. I would reach a peak from where I could look back and see how far I had already come. From up there I could look out on my world and see all the beautiful things far and near. But then with horrible speed, I would careen around a curve and plunge down into a valley. The bottom would drop out of my stomach as I clutched at the safety bar that broke loose in my hands. Cradled in the pit, I could see only the debris-littered ground and the puzzling structure supporting the whole elevated railway. The girders looked cracked and unstable and the long uphill climb ahead looked unmanageable.

In one of those dips, I thought about the day of the fire and wondered where my angel had been. When Shadrach, Meshach, and Abed-nego were thrown into the fiery furnace, God sent his angel to rescue these men who served and trusted him.[1] I had served and trusted God, but where was my angel?

In despair I had cried out, "I hate you, God. I hate you for letting this awful thing happen to me." The flames of my "why's" burned my insides.

When I related some of my agony to our friends Larry and Nancy Sayre one summer afternoon, telling them how I had literally screamed at God, Gene quietly said, "God wasn't threatened."

I never felt more loved by God than I did at that moment. As I reflected on what Gene said, I realized I felt no alienation from God. Even when I had vented all my rage on him that April night and at last crawled back into my bed, I had felt complete acceptance, as though he understood and my struggle was all right with him. And, yet, at the same time, I had felt guilty and ashamed for not having handled things better.

Later, it occurred to me to read again how Jesus faced his crucifixion. He wanted to run away, too. He felt betrayed and abandoned exactly as I did. He prayed, "Please, please let this cup pass from me."[2] And in the heat of his pain he had cried out, "Why . . . why . . . why . . . why have you forsaken me?"[3]

In the hospital during a dressing change, when I had moaned and my words ended in screams, everyone understood. They encouraged me to let it out, not to bottle it up inside. They were not threatened or persuaded to give up on me. To them, it was an important part of the healing process.

I came to believe that when my inner pain—the pain of being afraid and angry and ugly and oh, so lonely—became unendurable, it was all right to let it out. It was all a part of the healing of my spirit and God was not threatened.

I have found no answer to "Why?" People have cried it out in the midst of tragedy and crisis since time began and will, I believe, until all time ends. I know of no reason, no answer. We want a simple equation, a logical, almost scientific explanation for all of life. Finding none, some persons are filled with despair and give up. Others sing. Not necessarily because they have found an answer, but because they have a song. Some write their own songs; still others find God to be the author of their melody. The song God gave me to sing came through the fire edited but much clearer.

Lying around in the debris I uncovered many prayers, some my own, some belonging to other persons: "God, please heal my face, just my face. Don't let it be scarred, please."

"Please, God, let Mary Ellen live."

"I want to die, God. Please, just let me die."

"Grant complete healing, Lord."

These prayers and many others like them were prayed with sincere desires, yet from our human weakness, our ignorance. That I lived does not mean that some prayers were more powerful than others, or that there were more prayers for life than for a peaceful end to my suffering entered on the Great Tally Sheet in the sky.

The farmer prays for rain; the suburbanite for a nice day for a picnic. In a war, both sides may pray for victory. So what does an individual prayer accomplish?

I do not have any easy answers here; prayer takes us to the heart of the mystery in our relationship with God. I only know we are commanded to pray. In obedience we leave our concerns with God, and we trust the results to his care. I also know that God answers prayer.

In my case, many of these answers were given before any of us asked for them. Fine men and women had chosen the medical profession, invested years of their lives and a great deal of money in learning to be doctors and nurses. They then singled out burn technology as their specialized field. A good hospital made its burn unit a priority. These resources were made available minutes away from me when I needed them.

My own choices to exercise, eat well, not to smoke—all these gave my body a fighting chance. Sustaining relationships—friends we had made in each of Gene's churches—were formed. Even Dr. Yamaguchi acknowledged the power of their love as it began to flow from a small second-floor waiting room, down a corridor, through closed doors, and into a tank room.

Maybe that is, after all, the secret of how God works. Maybe he takes the ability of each of us to care about what happens to another human being and out of that kind of caring fashions the answers to our prayers.

Walking through the fire, I learned a lot about love, and yet, now I find it more mysterious, more undefinable, more awesome than ever before. You see, I have been loved back to life, and I'm not certain how it happened.

Within minutes after I was burned and jumped out my office window, a stranger was at my side. He could just as easily not have gotten involved. He could have driven on or, having come upon me in the alley, passed by on the other side. Did he love me? He didn't even know me!

Another person's caring took the shape of letters. Bill Cober is the executive director of the Board of National Ministries of the American Baptist Churches USA, a big title, but Bill is a big man and carries it well.

We had briefly met on one occasion when we had each expressed the loneliness of leaving the pastorate for denominational work. Based only on that moment of touching, he began to correspond when I was too sick to care or answer. Bill became my pastor and priest as he let me scream on paper. In my letters to him, I voiced all my despair and rage, and my feelings of betrayal and abandonment. There was never a word of reproach or recrimination, not one "You shouldn't feel that way." He just read my letters, and in reading, listened and accepted me where I was. From him I learned something.

In the past when anyone has raised questions about God I have felt compelled to come up with an answer. Bill didn't. Instead he heard me out, admitted he had a few unanswered questions himself, and in a sense, welcomed me to continue the search with him. Somehow it made me feel less afraid to be loved by this man and to know that not everyone in the upper echelon of my denomination had all his or her ducks sitting in a row, either.

Not one angel, but, instead, an entire community of believers came to protect me, to hold me up with their hands in my fiery furnace. I had wanted to die. Instead, there was this love that would not let me go. It began to weave a web of protection around me as my family gathered at Wishard Hospital. It grew as rapidly as the prayer chain. It was expressed in cards, letters, and gifts. There was this love that kept urging me to new life . . . to be born again, if you like.

I have been able to give words to some of my feelings about the power of love because of a book written by L. Robert Keck, *The Spirit of Synergy*.[4]

This book had lain on an end table in my living room since 1978, waiting for Gene to get around to reading it. I had picked it up, dusted it, and put it back in place. It wasn't until Bill Carson grabbed the book for something to read as he waited out my clinic visits each week that I finally noticed it. Robert Keck's book became one of the most useful items I carried out of the ashes. At one point Mr. Keck writes:

> My experience and the research I have cited simply illustrate the considerable evidence that God created us with a profound interrelationship. Intercessory prayer makes sense, and we can learn from a variety of research *how* we can improve our stewardship of this ability.
>
> Matthew 25: 34-45 expresses this interrelatedness very vividly for the Christian. Jesus points out here that all life is so interrelated that if we turn our back on a brother or sister in need, we turn our back on Him. Jesus reminded us of our undeniable interrelationship with one another and with Him.
>
> Meditative intercessory prayer, then, is a crucial dimension within the whole concept of prayer because it provides the channels through which we can send love, light, and health-giving energy—and receive the same.[5]

A man who suffered severe chronic pain, Robert Keck tells the story of his search for some relief from that pain. I devoured it, not once, but three or four times, and discovered in its pages ways I could constructively deal with my own pain.

The techniques were simple enough: relaxation, concentration, and imagery. I saw that I had already put these methods to work for me in a limited way. In the hospital when Ernie taught me a simple relaxation technique, I had begun to practice the art of letting go of stress. Concentration is really control over attention. When I had tried singing through my tankings for debridement, I was really diverting my attention away from pain to the words of a song. And as for imagery, I had vigorously exercised my imagination ever since I was a little girl.

The book picked up where Ernie had left off, adding the dimension of meditative prayer to the relaxation techniques. I began to practice the skills he suggested and soon found I was able to cope more constructively with constant pain, discomfort, and my inner anxieties about being disfigured. And, importantly, the techniques helped me to find relief at last from the itching that at times consumed me.

Predictably, I ran into barriers. The first was sleep. We have all practiced the art of relaxing prior to falling asleep. I had used the relaxation technique Ernie taught me in the hospital for this. Actually, I was using sleep as an escape from pain, not relaxation itself. I had to learn to relax body, mind, and spirit—and remain awake—before I could employ my deeply relaxed state as a time for prayer.

Up to this point in my burn experience, I had had tremendous difficulty in concentrating on anything. It wasn't so much a problem of my mind wandering, or of being distracted, as it was simply focusing in on something. It was a strange experience for me to sit for long periods of time and think nothing. It was as though my mind wandered in some vast gray area devoid of anything.

As I began to practice the concentration technique, perhaps by focusing my attention on a simple object (like an apple—considering the variations in color, the texture of the skin and stem), my mind began to respond much the same way as my atrophied muscles were responding to exercise. I gradually began to read again, watch television, and even follow a simple conversation. Later, I was able to utilize the acquired skill of concentration in meditative prayer as I began to draw on the power God had already created in me to creatively respond to my new body. And later still, I moved from practicing the three techniques—relaxation, concentration, and imagery—to using them in a form of prayer new to me.

As Mr. Keck had suggested in his book, I recorded the prayers I used on a cassette in a "very relaxed, slow, and soft voice."[6] I began by using one of his examples:

> First read Psalm 8.
> Now, just allow yourself to relax very deeply, relaxing in body, mind, and spirit, allowing yourself to let go of all the stress and tension that we carry with us physiologically, psychologically, spiritually, and just trusting in the presence of God in the very depths of your being.
> Because of the close interrelationship of your body, mind, and spirit, if you just think "relaxation," you will begin to move in that direction. In your consciousness, now, feel or see your feet and your ankles and feel them beginning to relax, let go—becoming very loose and limp—very, very, deeply relaxed. As those muscles relax, you are just letting the stress and tension flow out, away from your body.[7]

When each part of my body had been thought about and consciously relaxed, I spent as long as I liked enjoying the lightness and freedom that I was experiencing. Then I moved on to the very core of the experience—the goal of all the techniques—communion with my God.

> Imagine that you are out on a lazy summer day, hiking along a riverbank. From time to time you pause to study the detail of wild flowers or of the water's edge. Be aware of the trees, the dirt, the rocks, the breeze. Feel very much attuned to the nature that is all about you. . . .
> The God who created this universe is here, present—in your life. You are related

to all that you see. You are a special,
unique, original creation of God. Sense the
awe, the wonder. Now, pick out a star and
follow the light of that star, coming to earth,
right down to you there looking at it. That
light enters and touches your body—moving down deep into every minute cell of
your body—where God's spirit is the creative and sustaining force. Let yourself bask
in the sense of your uniqueness and your
participation in the vastness of the universe.
Experience the awe and wonder and your
special place in being at home with the God
that has created all of the universe—being
loved . . . being accepted . . . just as you are
. . . with no need to earn God's love. Just
be—for you are loved. Bask in this communion with God for a period of time. Let
yourself fully experience it.

Then after a while, knowing that you
can return to this spot again if you would
like, begin to leave this spot, carrying with
you the sense of being accepted just as you
are and appreciating the vastness of the universe. Carry that feeling with you as you
begin gradually to let your awareness return
to a surface state of consciousness—back to
external, physical reality.[8]

As I used the power of imagery to return again and
again to that shady, cool riverbank and felt again the *at-one-
ment* with God, I began to realize that the I that is really me
had made it through the fire. A little singed around the
edges, maybe, but with no lasting crippling effects.

One night during the time I was heavily into a particular
meditative prayer, I had a curious dream. I'm not one to pay
much attention to dreams—there are only a few I even

remember the following morning—but this one intrigued me. In the dream, I was sleeping in my own bed, in my own bedroom—everything was very familiar—when I heard a voice calling my name. I got up, seeming to know the voice came from outside the house, and stepped out onto the front porch. I knew where the voice was coming from and walked down the street to the corner, turned and headed toward Holiday Park, just a block away. The voice—never growing any louder—continued to call me by name. The park was cast in the pink shades of a late spring sunset. It occurred to me that this was strange because the park lay to the east of our home, not the west. As I walked toward the crest of the ravine that drops to the White River, I was enveloped by the pink aura. And then I noticed that in the pink light, my scars were not visible.

I woke up then. It was morning. Gene, disturbed by my stirrings, opened his eyes and turned toward me. When I had finished telling him my dream, he said, "It was a beautiful dream, wasn't it?"

I exhaled a breathless, "Yes."

One might say God used a dream to tell me that I was more than a body and that the closer I walked toward him, the less my scars would matter to me. Or, you might say it was only a dream, the subconscious wishful fantasizing of a distraught lady. You may take your pick. I took mine.

Robert Keck's book turned into a mirror, reflecting back at me not the ugliness of my body but some images of the person within. I began my own little ritual. Each time I went into the bathroom, I looked into a small mirror hanging on the wall and said, "I am special. I am unique. I am still God's child. I am loved." Over and over I repeated the same phrases, sometimes with tears coursing down my cheeks, sometimes with sarcasm. But always I tried to outshout the image in the mirror that taunted me, "Beauty is only skin deep . . . but ugly goes clear to the bone."

Slowly I began to reconstruct my OK-ness. It was there in the ashes in my trunk. I first packed it when I worked so hard on my self-image during our crisis with our daughter, Jill. I had taken it out and worn it when my marriage appeared to be threatened, although it didn't seem to fit very well then. It needed to be restyled now before it could be worn to good advantage again.

I realized how much of my OK-ness had been fashioned out of my good looks and what I was able to do, rather than the fabric of who I was. It was a major job, but I had learned how to make alterations long before the fire.

One day, something blew up out of the ashes quite unexpectedly. Gene and I had contacted Upjohn Health-care Services again, this time for some homemaker assistance. Keeping up with the housework had become more than Gene could handle, and I was still unable to do very much. So Angie came to help us. That night as Marinel did my dressing change I very solemnly said, "Some people will do *anything* to get out of doing housework."

"Mary Ellen," she said, amazed, "that's the first time I've heard you joke about what's happened to you."

It was a simple key, but it unlocked a big door that led to a lot of healing. What a gift laughter is! It smooths off the sharp edges so things don't cut as much.

It enabled Marinel to ask, "Do you ever watch Star Trek? You could get a job as Dr. Spock's wife."

I knew what she meant: parts of my ears were burned off, leaving them pointed like Dr. Spock's. We both giggled.

Jill had asked if there wasn't some way Gene and I could help our son, Joe, accept what had happened to me. "Mom, I know you have a lot to handle, but Joe is really having a bad time with this. When he comes home from Indy, he can't talk about seeing you without choking up."

As the family joker, Joe had picked up the habit of referring to Gene as "young man" and to me as "woman." It is easy to see where it came from. Whenever Gene reprimanded the boys, he would preface his remarks with, "Young man . . . ."

And when I was about to share from my vast store of

wisdom with three sons who towered over me, Joe would say, "Woman . . . sit down." It was a fun kind of repartee we all enjoyed. Letters were even delivered addressed to "Young Man and Woman Ton." There had always been a lot of craziness and laughter in our lives together. Always, until the fire. Then, suddenly, nothing was funny. Nothing was even neutral. Everything was morbid.

We all needed to laugh again, but especially Joe. So the very next time he came, I said to him, "Joe, get this old, crippled lady a pillow, will you?"

Joe looked startled as he went to get the pillow for my back. Later in the day when I hobbled out into the kitchen, he said, "Sit down, old, crippled lady before you fall down." Laughter filled the kitchen. It was more nourishing than the lunch we ate.

I began to refer to myself as "The World's Only Human Roasted Hot Dog," and the kids joked about the "crazy lady who kept walking around the house and backyard carrying two purses." One day Vicki joined me out back. "I just thought I'd better walk with you," she said, "to keep you from jumping the fence."

My son, Jack, was able to comment to some friends, "If you think it's weird my mother carries her purse around, you should see what's in it." He opened it to show the Campbell soup cans I used to add extra weight to pull my arms back down to their normal position at my sides.

"For everything there is a season and a time for every matter under heaven: a time to weep, and a time to laugh."[9]

I had started laughing on the outside to help Joe, inside I was still crying. But I learned something: laughter dries many of the tears.

There is nothing that I ever did, or could yet do, to deserve the kind of love I experienced. That's grace! God's grace, as it came to me through his people.

A beautifully embroidered quilt came from the Edna

Martin Circle in Evansville. Each lady had done the hand-
work on one square, signed her name, and carefully
stitched it with floss. For me, it was symbolic of all the
persons who had entered our lives during the past year.
Each one had chosen her own design and the color of her
caring, and then set to work sewing it into the fabric of our
lives.

How could I continue to deny that I was still a person,
loved and cherished? How deny that I was a unique and
special child of God when God's people put on a demon-
stration like that?

And so . . . I reached for life.

15

What's a Nice Girl like Me Doing in a Body like This?

I had heard of kids growing too big for their britches, but I had never heard of anyone being too big for his skin. This was precisely what I felt like. It seemed as though my skin had shrunk, and there was no longer enough elasticity to allow me to move about. My arms still wouldn't hang down at my sides or reach up over my head. Bending over or stooping down was a painful process, which might send me sprawling. My neck wouldn't turn. My face was so tight that any movement distorted my mouth and eyes. People continued to sympathetically ask, "Are you still in very much pain?"

Rather than crybaby all the time, I stole the perfect response from a television show, "No, only when I am sitting, standing, or lying down!"

It wasn't just that my body felt too big for my skin. My spirit was cramped, too. I had plans and hopes and dreams that would not be contained in my scarred, broken body. I still hated that body, hated everything about it: the lack of mobility, the inability to use my hands, the pain—but, most of all, the scars that each day were painted more vividly and permanently upon me. I had roles to play that this costume simply didn't fit: career woman, executive's wife, speaker. No way could I ever make a public appearance looking like this.

My spirit still rode that emotional roller coaster. I listened to my mother-in-law telling me about a family in their church whose home had burned. She spoke of their pain and grief and told me they had lost everything. My immediate response was, "Everything? They've lost nothing! They are all alive and no one was so much as touched by the fire."

But, later, as I reflected back on the incident, I realized my emotional outburst had been off base. Of course, they were well aware of their good fortune and thankful to be alive and unharmed. But they had suffered a real loss. A home is more than a house—it's a place where we belong. Countless memories are stored there, not to mention all the momentos acquired through the years that are a graphic, pictorial history of the lives lived there. In a real sense, they suffered the visible loss of their past and must feel rootless.

I could identify with that loss completely. My body was the home I had lived in for forty-six years. Looking at it now, I felt devastated by the loss of everything familiar, just as that family must have felt as they wandered through the wreckage of their house. There had been beautiful memories stored in that home of mine. Memories of walking down a corridor, heels clicking on the tile, and turning a male head or two. Memories of dressing up for a celebration with Gene and feeling as Maria did when she sang in *West Side Story,* "I feel pretty. I feel pretty. I feel pretty and witty and wise." There were memories of swimming and playing volleyball and working all spring to acquire a suntan. And, always, there were the memories of making love.

Just like that family, I was lucky to be alive. I knew that and at times rejoiced. But, also just like that family, not a day passed that I was not in some way confronted with what I had lost.

As if my body wasn't bad enough, on June 2 my Jobst arrived. The Jobst or Jobskin is a custom-made pressure garment.[1] Its purpose is to minimize the excessive growth of scar tissue during that time when the scar is maturing. While I was still hospitalized, exacting measurements had been taken from the top of my head to my toes so a Jobst garment could be constructed to my specific size and shape. This brown, elastic leotard, turtleneck jacket, and face mask was to function as my first layer of skin normally would have, applying pressure to the underlayer.

When skin is severely burned into the second layer, it loses the benefit of the tight skin pressure that was once on top. This underlayer then grows wild as it tries to heal and form a scar. Little threadlike elements in the second layer contribute to the strength of the body covering, much like filaments in heavy-duty, package-wrapping tape. If no pressure is applied to these elements, they tend to grow and form irregular knots, swirls, and other strange shapes that cause the skin surface to scar grotesquely.

The little instruction booklet that comes with each part of the Jobst garment does not mention the pain involved in pulling these tight therapeutic devices on over newly healed skin. It only casually mentions the possibility of blisters forming or new skin being rubbed off, leaving raw areas to heal all over again. Nor does it allude in any way to the psychological trauma in the mind of the burn victim when a body, already having endured a nightmare of pain, is now subjected to further torture.

For me there was tremendous mental anguish each time I struggled into my Jobst. I cannot entirely explain the myriad feelings that knotted my stomach and bludgeoned my psyche. I felt torn between allowing my body to heal naturally and voluntarily inflicting more pain on it for the sake of flattening a few scars.

"What's the difference whether I have bumpy scars or flat scars?" I complained to Gene. "Scars are still scars after all. No matter what I do, I am scarred for life."

But the therapists at the hospital, the doctors, Gene, my good friends—they all said, "Wear it, you'll be sorry if you don't." All of them seemed to feel that they knew what was best for me. But not one of them had been burned or worn a compression garment; even my friend David, who had been burned, had opted not to wear his.

I tried. I really tried. But one day when my mother told me, "You are making choices that will affect the rest of your life; you don't want to decide not to do something now you will regret later," I responded from deep down in my gut with words I didn't know were even a part of me, "Bull ----!" The swear words shot out of me and exploded in the air, surprising me as much as they did my mother. There was a long moment of silence from the other end of the telephone line, and then the conversation was hastily terminated.

My new vocabulary both shamed and puzzled me. Swearing had never been a part of my life-style, but somewhere along the road to recovery it crept in, when, in utter frustration and exasperation over my ineptness, I vented the tangle of feelings within me. Using profanity with someone else made me realize the kind of habit I was cultivating. But, I realized something else, too. The expletives were spewing out a lot of the pent-up anger that I had been trying to release in torrents of tears. Although my tears had a way of temporarily relieving some of the emotional pressure building up, they were a dead-end street. My anger, which I had always kept hidden out back in the alleys of my life, was pushing me toward the main street where life flowed. Those two words propelled me further along my way than any tears had ever done.

I hung up the phone and sat in the light green, corduroy chair I had reupholstered for our bedroom. The bright sunlight was coming in between the flowered drapes that I had sewn and lit up the needlepoint wall hanging I had done. This room, this whole house, was full of me: furniture I had stripped and refinished, chairs and couches I had reupholstered, pictures I had embroidered or creweled, plants I had cultivated from leaf cuttings, closets full of clothes I had sewn. From front door to screened-in porch this home bore my mark.

"It's not fair . . . it's not fair," I shouted to the empty rooms. And words I had spoken to my own children resounded back at me, "Whoever told you life was fair?" The implication was that they were to rise above the unfairness, injustice, and childhood calamities that befell them.

"I don't want to live like this," I cried again. And this time it was Gene's words that replayed: "But, you didn't die. You lived. You are alive whether you want to be or not. You can become bitter and ugly inside or you can fight back. It's up to you. No one can do it for you."

It was my anger that brought me up out of that chair, pushed me into the kitchen, and started me setting the table for dinner. One plate at a time, one spoon at a time, one knife on the floor to stay there until Gene could retrieve it. Back and forth I went between table and cupboards and drawers. I finished my first major undertaking by using fingers that hurt whenever they touched anything and hands that clumsily scooped up plates to be carried between my palms.

Gene's, "Hey, babe, look what you did!" crowned my accomplishment.

At dinner I explained to him, "I'm not going to wear those Jobst garments right now. I have scars you can't see, ones that are inside. I need to take time to heal those first. If I'm all healed and flat outside, but there's nothing left of me,' where will I be then?"

There were a lot of people who knew what was best for the outside of me on a long-term basis. But, I had to take it one day at a time. Get through today and then see about tomorrow.

It was also my anger that gave me the determination to get in the car and drive myself to the clinic. It was anger that had me chasing a slippery potato all over the kitchen floor until I succeeded in peeling it. Through it all, I came to recognize my anger as neither right nor wrong—but simply a God-given emotion like any other to be used constructively or destructively.

By August I began to exercise with a passion. There were a number of simple exercises I had been encouraged to do right along, and I had done them, mechanically going through the motions. It was agony to push hard enough so that the range of motion of my hands, arms, and neck would improve.

Now I rediscovered something I had always known: anger gives the body strength. Years ago a newspaper had carried an article about a "giant" black man who raised the metal cab of an overturned truck off its driver. With his bare hands, he had pulled out the brake pedal, which trapped the driver's foot. He had beaten out the flames in the cab with nothing but his hands. Later, Charles Dennis Jones, who was six feet tall, hardly a giant, explained: "I hate fire." Months before, his child had burned to death in his home.

I also hated, only what I hated was my own body! I determined to make the best possible use of my anger. I began to push against the pain. To push and push and push. From the two empty purses I had started carrying to pull my arms down, I had gradually worked up to a bar of Ivory soap in each one, and then to three Campbell's soup cans. Now I discarded the purse to use a heavier weight, a gallon milk jug filled with water.

Gene tied a piece of plastic tubing (this resembled a hose, but was very soft and spongy) to the handle of the jug with a piece of clothesline so it would be more tolerable for my hands. I wore a path in the grass walking around the backyard. Then I began to follow the maze left behind by the swipes of the power lawn mower. Back and forth, up and down the yard I journeyed, toting my jug, sweating and hurting. But my arms began to fall back into a more natural position at my sides.

From the bottom of a dresser drawer, I resurrected an old copy of the Royal Canadian Air Force's *Guide to Physical Fitness*;[2] from a mail-order house, I ordered a body shaper,[3] a simple exercising device using ropes and pulleys. Bill and Claribel Carson loaned me their exercise bike, and I set to work. The most important part of my day became the time I spent exercising. At first, I could barely pedal for five minutes and then had to take a nap to recuperate. For months, the sheet I spread on the floor to work out on was spotted with blood where new skin rubbed off under the pressure or a too-tightly healed juncture pulled apart. But I was driven by my own anger to stick with it.

Slowly, very slowly, my body began to respond. Each passing week the pain decreased and I moved more freely. I could get up out of my chair without pushing off with my arms. I stopped shuffling and walked with spirit. I could get in and out of the car with comparative ease, and miracle of miracles, I could turn on my side, curl up, and go to sleep. After sleeping for months flat and rigid on my back, this was scrumptious.

By the middle of August, I had put my Jobst back on. I had been wearing the leotard for some time but not the jacket or face mask. There certainly is no funnier sight than Gene helping me into those elastic long johns. The intricacies of panty hose are foreign to most men. Even when I had taught him all I knew, my leotards still came out with the seams on the side and crotch opening off base. When he pulled up on them, my feet always left the floor at the same time. The day did come when we even laughed at this.

In full regalia, I could have doubled for Mork's sister—or some other character from outer space. Every time I looked in the mirror I was reminded of the monkey dolls Jill had made out of a brown cotton stocking. The tightness of the face mask even caused my lips to protude in apelike fashion. Or, as someone once said, "You look like you're puckered up for a big kiss."

The Jobst garments were monstrously uncomfortable and broke open fresh areas on my elbows, shoulders, underarms, face, and ears. But this time I was as determined as the pain; I used both the aggressiveness of my anger and the passiveness of relaxation techniques to hold out. The anger, so long pent up inside me, was slowly, constructively being dissipated.

I had taken charge of my body again. A long time ago,

lying in the dirt of an alley, I had given it to others. Now I was ready to claim my body as my own. It didn't hurt my feelings one bit to watch the pregnantlike belly I had come home with disappear or to hear Gene remark as he put his hands on my waist, "You're as slender as you were before the babies."

But there was still my face to deal with.

We all know it's the inner person that matters. . . . What we look like outside isn't important. I had been reminded of that many times by friends and acquaintances. But when the comment was casually made to me one day by an attractive woman as she carefully rearranged a few stray wisps of hair and applied fresh lipstick, I had a strong urge to ask her if she would like to change places with me. I knew she could not have glibly spouted that trite expression if she lived in my skin for even one minute.

When well-meaning friends had come to see me for the first time, it was much like they were calling at a funeral home. Not knowing what to say when they saw my scarred body, they resurrected inane cliches like those uttered at a mortuary. "She looks so beautiful." "He looks as though he's sleeping." "My, doesn't Aunt Tillie look well?" And, later, other comments meant to be helpful are made. "How lucky you are to have two other children!" "You're so young; you'll marry again some day." "Better he should have died quickly and unexpectedly than to suffer." All of these remarks are about as helpful as the doctor's advice, "Take two aspirins and go to bed," when you are suffering from the flu.

Similarly inappropriate phrases came at me over and over, and they stung. I knew people meant well. I understood their confusion and helplessness, but I didn't want to hear "Beauty is only skin deep." Or "Beauty comes from within." If just one of those comments had come from a crippled, deformed, or disfigured person, I might have been able to be receptive. But they came from women who had obviously taken great pains to style their hair, apply their makeup, and shop for their clothes. Or from carefully shaven men, who smelled of Brut, wore good-looking suits, and had their hair cut in a style shop. Or from persons who had opted for contact lenses or a shell to cover a blind eye.

It wasn't that I needed friends to commiserate with me, I just wanted someone to understand what it meant to be suddenly and irrevocably robbed of all physical comeliness. A face is the key to our identity. When we walk into a room, it is our face that draws others to us. Everyone has experienced the embarrassment of running up to a familiar-looking back, only to be confronted by a strange face when the person turns.

A few persons admitted that perhaps I didn't look too good right now, *but* . . . . "But I know someone who was burned or in a bad accident and today they look as good as ever."

"But not enough time has gone by. Give it time. Time is a burn's best friend."

"But they can do miracles with plastic surgery now."

These persons wanted to hold hope out to me, because they really couldn't resolve their own feelings unless they could believe I would be all right again. I wanted to believe that, too, but, at the core of my being, I knew I had to accept the fact that I was going to be permanently disfigured. To build my new life on the sands of false hope would mean I would have to start all over again when the inevitable tide washed away the sand castle.

There was a lot of guilt over my preoccupation with my appearance. I began to berate myself for being so vain and foolish. After all, I was alive, I told myself, and I should be grateful for that. Nothing else mattered.

But it did matter!

Marty, the social service worker in the burn unit, picked up some of my distress signals and brought me a book to read from the medical library, *The Emotional Care of the Facially Burned and Disfigured.*[4] Just the fact that someone had written a book with such a purpose said a lot to me. I was feeling so singled out, so very different and isolated. Here was a book devoted to understanding persons who had faced tragedies similar to mine. I discovered two things: first, I was not just being vain and foolish; I was involved in a recognized emotional crisis. And second, there were persons with far worse burns than I could even have imagined.

The book did not answer any of my "How?" questions: How do I live like this? How do I relate to others? How, in a world where beauty is god, do I survive? But it did identify the problem and give words to my feelings:

> While inner values have consistently spoken in a quiet and spiritual voice, the louder and more insistent focus on surfaces can nowhere better be seen than in our current society, with its preoccupation with beauty culture. The creams, lotions, diets, exercises and rituals keep changing, but the din in the salons and the supermarkets is a steady one, demanding increasing effort and expense, presuming that attractiveness enhances basic worth. Orthodontics in the suburbs has long been an accepted procedure, largely done to enhance the acceptability of our children. For more and more people rhinoplasty is as acceptable as dieting. Today surgeons are besieged with requests to enlarge, trim and shape breasts. Operations to remove fat, erase scars, lift sagging chins, remove pouches under the eyes, and fill in cavernous cheeks are all common; and the details of applying eye shadow, powdering, coloring the lips and lining and plucking the eyebrows and the limits of naturalness in appearance all rapidly fluctuate. More men than ever are having

their faces lifted. The goal is to make people more aesthetically and sexually attractive through diligent work on their appearance.[5]

Of course, an elemental truth was spoken by friends who reassured me that beauty lies in the eye of the beholder. But the culture we are a part of speaks so loudly I couldn't hear what they were saying. This pressure rests heavy on us all. We can't grow old, have gray hair, or wrinkles—not even "brown spots." Pimples aren't allowed, fat is abhorred, and we shouldn't even smell like human beings.

Something is wrong in our world when the *Ladies Home Journal* writes about tv actress Loni Anderson, " . . . admittedly insecure about her looks, Loni wouldn't dream of setting foot outside the front door, even to go to the corner drugstore, without being thoroughly made up and ready to face her public."[6] Her husband, Ross Bickell says, " . . . Loni needs constant assurance."[7] Under this kind of tension, why are we incredulous when beauty queens commit suicide, or, faced with the inevitable, unrelenting ticking of the clock, turn to alcohol and/or drugs? If even the Loni Andersons are insecure, where does that leave you? And where does it leave me?

The church has also succumbed to the pressure. I had sat in a church business meeting one night when one of the most important items on the list of a pastoral candidate's qualifications was his "beautiful blonde wife" and his own tall and handsome appearance. "A couple the church could be proud to represent them," it had said. In yet another instance a pastor was rejected by a church because his wife was too fat. If there is still doubt in your mind, browse in a Christian bookstore. Martin Marty once asked, after looking over a long shelf of Christian books by the Anita Bryants and Pat Boones, "Where are the books about fat girls with pimples who sit in wheelchairs?"

During the time of my convalescence, I viewed the triumph of Roy Campanella on my television screen. Campanella—baseball star of the late 50s and early 60s—made a heroic effort to reestablish his life after a tragic automobile accident left him a quadriplegic. I also watched a paraplegic girl learn to fly an airplane, and Helen Keller to sign and speak. Through the miracle of cinema, I watched Joni Eareckson relive her drama in the film simply titled *Joni*. Almost completely paralyzed, Joni today is a well-known artist and speaker. Each of these films spoke to me, as they did to others, of the indomitability of the human spirit in the face of tremendous handicaps. "But, where," I asked myself, "are stories about disfigured persons?" By their very absence, the die is cast, the jury already in, and the verdict given, guilty . . . guilty of being ugly.

My book on disfigurement gave a reason for society's ostracism of the disfigured:

> Many of the terrified reactions to marked disfigurement seem to resemble the traditional terror and revulsion that people manifest toward lepers. While the disfigured do not seem automatically infectious there is a dread of touching them and coming near them, as if some of the damage can be caught or spread. The tactile image is exaggerated; touching a scar is hardly a strange feeling but it is dreaded, like touching a snake viewed as slimy though snakes are quite dry. Confrontation with a damaged face disrupts the sense of inner security and confident self-esteem of daily life. Our feeling that we are getting on all right is momentarily sundered by a sight we treat as a physical threat.[9]

What we do not understand, we tend to ignore. We understand little about *ugly* except that it is bad. From childhood on we read of the ugly stepsisters who are mean and cruel, ugly witches who cast horrible spells on people, and stepmothers who disguise themselves as ugly, old hags as a ploy in their devious plots. Makeup artists skillfully apply scars, open wounds, and distorted features on the faces of the "bad guys" in films. This stigma is the lot of the disfigured. We are society's deviants.

There are exceptions. Under certain circumstances being ugly is OK . . . if you are a man. Beauty loved the Beast and the beautiful princess did kiss the ugly (male) frog. Is there a fairy tale about a female beast who is loved in spite of her ugliness? And where are the female counterparts to the not-so-attractive actors like Walter Matthau, Humphrey Bogart, or Telly Savalas? We have been so indoctrinated we don't even think of these men as homely; women think they are "cute." But their leading ladies are usually younger and always attractive, if not beautiful. Men *may* be allowed to be homely, even ugly, *if* they have other compensatory attributes. I saw the movie *Elephant Man,* but if there are any female "elephants," I think we will never see them on film.

To be deviant (when we think of deviance we mean permanent differences that are never fashionable) in a culture that worships beauty is terribly hurtful; to be deviant and female is to know inexpressible agony. Please don't tell me to take two aspirins and go to bed.

16

He Loves Me . . .
He Loves Me Not

The first time I spoke to a women's group about my journey through the fire I jokingly told them, "Any woman going to bed dressed from head to toe in a Jobst doesn't need a headache." They laughed knowingly and so did I. The time had come to laugh, even at that aspect of my journey. But, the tremendous adjustment Gene and I had to make as man and woman, husband and wife, had led through a time of deep mourning.

I had come home from the hospital convinced that Gene could not possibly want me for his wife any longer. I knew that no man was ever going to give me a second look or consider me an attractive woman again. On a scale of 1 to 10, I didn't even make the scoreboard.

It didn't help to read the statistics. Over half of burn victims' marriages end in divorce. The books I read admitted readily to the myriad problems confronting burn victims and their spouses, but offered no positive reinforcement. They seemed instead to imply that the problem was magnified when facial disfigurement was involved. My mind continually returned to a paragraph in Dr. Bernstein's book, *Emotional Care of the Facially Burned and Disfigured.*

> Husbands and wives do not readily bring
> up sexual problems related to disfigure-

ment, but this is one more area of readjust-
ment. One husband who took scrupulous
care of his wife said, "I feel like vomiting
when I think of sex with her."[1]

To think that Gene might feel this way about me hurt
deeply and saddened me, too. That sadness permeated our
relationship as, in effect, I began to apologize for living. I
offered him his freedom. "No one who sees me could
possibly blame you for leaving," I told him. "In some ways,
I would be better off, too. I feel my ugliest with you."

In my heart I knew he would never walk out on me, not
now; the fire had welded him into our marriage. His code of
ethics would not permit him to free himself. I was certain he
must feel imprisoned in a hopeless situation.

But I seriously underestimated the man I have been
married to for twenty-nine years.

I realize as I write this chapter that many different
persons will read it. Some will find it offensive. I am reminded of a dear old lady who was a guest in my home in
Evansville. Many of the ladies in the group had never seen
the inside of their parsonage, and I invited them to take a
tour. After "oohing" and "ahhing" over Jill's room and
remarking "how pretty" the master bedroom was, several
stopped as they looked into Jack's room. Little statues,
banners, books, and a stuffed Snoopy on the bed gave sure
evidence of his feeling about the Peanuts gang. Gene liked
the cartoon strip himself and often used it as sermon illustra-
tions. With great delight, the lady said: "And *this* must be
Reverend Ton's room!"

If you are a person who thinks ministers have their own
private bedrooms and will be disillusioned to discover that
the stork did not bring their children to the rooftop of the
parsonage, please turn to the next chapter. But for the others
who walk—or may walk—where Gene and I are walking, I
wish to share that part of our struggle.

When I worked up all my courage and voiced some of

my anxiety over our sexual relationship to my doctor, he referred me to one of the nurses, who in turn wrote down the name and telephone number of a mental health clinician. Needless to say, I never called the number. I guess I expected another referral and another stranger's admittance into a personal area of my life. Now, I believe their reluctance to handle the problem was their own bewilderment. They had no answers, no suggestions; they hadn't walked where we were walking.

Gene had consistently assured me of his love when I was in the hospital, and I was too engaged in a life-and-death struggle to question it. He would come and stand or sit near my bed, sometimes drifting off to sleep as I did, and it was enough just to be near one another.

Then one night just before visiting hours ended at 8:00, he had bent over and kissed me on my crusty lips. The conflict—still not ended, even as I write—had begun within me. I wanted his touch, needed his kiss, and yet, I was repulsed. Not by him, but by myself. I was appalled at the very thought of giving myself to him like this.

When I had returned home, Gene cared for me gently and tenderly, much as a mother cares for her baby. But it was the wrong role for both of us. He began to speak to others about me in my presence, saying things like, "She has a lot of pain," or "She can't shake your hand."

It both humiliated and infuriated me. I did not want to be this man's child; I wanted to be his wife.

Gene would assure me that my appearance did not bother him or "turn him off." But as the weeks turned into months and the soreness began to leave my body, and still he did not make any overtures, I found that impossible to believe.

At first he had blamed the fact that I was too sore to touch. Then it was the twin beds we slept in. When we finally returned to our own room and our own bed, he was too tired. I told him once it was a wife's prerogative to be tired, not his.

Of course, we were playing games with each other. We had both lost something that had been very precious to us—my body—and we grieved the loss in many ways. Gene did not grow up unaffected by a culture that equates physical attractiveness with love and sex. Neither did I. Nor had we received any shots to ward off the attack on our subconscious by Madison Avenue. We had been wholly immersed in the media's propaganda as to what is beautiful and lovable and, if you will, what is sexy. We had to build up our own antibodies to fight off the infection.

Small things that happened during the course of the day would send me spiraling downward into a pit of self-abasement. Like the morning in July when I had first pulled open my dresser drawer. Lying there, all neatly folded, were my pretty nighties: soft pastels, spaghetti straps, covered with lace. Even when our income was meager, I had found money to buy a lovely nightgown. No pajamas or cotton nightshirts for me! Many times when Gene came home from a business trip, he would pull out of his suitcase a sheer, frilly bit-of-almost-nothing he had bought. It seemed important for us to have this symbol that we were more than a mother and father; we were also a man and woman in love with each other.

I wore as a badge of honor the fact that in all our married life I had never just flopped into bed, but rather prepared for it like I was going out, carefully bathing, brushing my hair, and selecting a nightgown. Gene could identify every different fragrance of perfume I owned. Always we had protected this as a special time for us. When the children grew into their teens and many parents grow nervous and uneasy about this aspect of their relationship, Gene and I felt the best sex education we could give them was the knowledge that their mother and father were lovers, too.

That day in July when I looked at each nightie in the drawer and then into the big mirror that hung over the dresser, the pain had washed over me in huge waves. I had never felt my ugliness as I did then.

For a long while, it seemed that every television commercial, every magazine advertisement, was a lever to pry loose the fragile glue holding together the shattered pieces of my sexuality. Even as I occupied my customary chair in the corner of the clinic waiting room, turning pages listlessly in an outdated magazine, the words jumped off the page battering against me . . .

FOR BETTER OR FOR WORSE, HOW DOES YOUR HUSBAND SEE YOU NOW?

Under those words, printed in large, black caps, as if it was necessary to repeat its assault for emphasis, the ad continued:

> No woman expects to look as young as she did the day she said "I do." Still, when you remember the look in your husband's eyes, you wonder how he sees you now.

Not me! I didn't wonder. I knew. I was certain he must look at me and feel like throwing up just like the husband in Bernstein's book.

Even the pages of the *Indianapolis Star* screamed at me, with a headline:

> Beauty Only Epidermis Deep.[2]

The author declared that mottled skin detracted from a woman's charm.

And on the facing page I read Ann Landers's column, wholeheartedly agreeing with a reader who could not fathom why any woman would allow herself to have gray hair. "Beats me," was Ann's response. "Maybe some are marching to a different drummer."[3]

These daily confrontations seemed to undermine my

best efforts to salvage some small vestige of my womanliness.

As I tormented myself with thoughts of unworthiness, I sank deeper into depression. In that frame of mind, I cut myself further off from Gene. When I told him I felt ugly with him, didn't want to be married to him anymore, he became sad: "You're not ugly to me." Or defensive: "I'm doing the best I can. I don't know how else to respond to you." Or angry: "Why can't you just accept the fact that I love you and help me?"

But it was incomprehensible to me that Gene could still love me; I was so thoroughly brainwashed by a culture that emphatically stated love was synonymous with body beauty. Whoever read a love story where the heroine is anything but beautiful? She never has a problem with coarse hair, dry skin, or teeth that are not perfectly aligned. Nor is she slightly overweight. How then, by any stretch of the imagination, could I be considered lovable?

My skin was thick and bumpy; my fingers were twisted and stiff with some of the nails missing; my trunk was striped with multiple scars where donor skin had been cut off. I looked for all the world like a crazy patchwork quilt.

Time and time again, I said to Gene, "You couldn't possibly love me now."

And time and time again, he responded, "I do love you, Mary. Why can't you believe that?"

"Because I think you confuse pity with love." I was convinced of that.

Then one day, quite by accident, he hit upon the magic formula. "What if it were me? What if I was the one who had been burned? How would you feel?"

My too quick response was, "I don't know. I don't know how I would feel." But the question sent the wheels of my imagination in motion, wheels that eventually eased my way up to the top of the hill and allowed me a glimpse of my "promised land."

What if it was Gene? I thought. In my mind I saw him

burned raw and bleeding. I saw him in the tank having the skin torn off his body. I saw him with no hair, scabs, and oozing sores, and my heart cried out in protest and my love for him sweat blood. I saw him stripped of all his manliness and pride. In my agony I wanted only one thing: that he would know I loved him. There were no boundaries, no limits to my love.

This fantasy, conjured up at will, was the sole thing that gave some credence to the incredible thought that I might still be loved.

But, when Gene would try to approach me with a gentle hug or a tender kiss, I would respond, "Don't! Please, don't. You don't have to do that." Then later I would reproach him with words from one of Ann Murray's discs, "We don't make love anymore." It was a no-win situation.

Marriage counselors readily agree that sex is not the most important ingredient in a couple's relationship. And I would echo, "Right! It's not." Until you can't. Suddenly it becomes most important and becomes the coatrack on which all else hangs.

As I began to write this book, I lamented to Gene, "I guess I will either not write about our relationship—just ignore it like it wasn't an important factor—or, admit that what experts have already written is true: 'It is difficult, if not impossible, for a marriage to survive fire.' "

Looking back, there were at least two decisive things that began to effect a change.

First, there was Green Lake. A good friend of Gene's offered to let us use his home on our American Baptist Assembly grounds at Green Lake, Wisconsin. Strange how things happen sometimes. Gene had been at Green Lake for the board meetings of our denomination in June and he had stayed at the Bordens' home. One evening as he walked down the hill to the dining hall, he became aware of how very relaxed he felt. Realizing how much he had needed this time away from the pressures of the past months, Gene thought how great it would be if both he and I could return together. *Perhaps in the fall,* he thought, *when Mary Ellen is stronger and it is cooler.*

No sooner had Gene entered the lobby of the dining hall that June night, than Stan Borden had approached him and suggested that the two of us would be welcome to use his home. I don't think Gene ever related to Stan exactly how amazed he was.

When Gene told me about it, I said, "No way. You've got to be kidding; look at me." But, despite my firm protest, the middle of October found us on our way to Green Lake.

It was a beautiful time for us both: a growing-together-again time. We rode bikes and walked in the woods, romped with Muffie and spent long evenings in front of the fireplace talking. Sometimes our talk left the fire and went to our children, other times spent at Green Lake, our little grandsons, or home improvements we would like to make. And we talked about the incredible love we had experienced during the last eight months.

We ate and we walked and we talked. We slept and rose again and watched the sun rise and set. We took deep, deep breaths of the calm we felt in the woods and saw reflected in the water. And we felt like two ordinary, normal people again.

Then I could no longer quote Ann Murray's song. I discovered that wasn't the crux of the problem at all. I had blamed everything on the absence of sexual intercourse. It didn't lie there. I should have known that. Our marriage was more than that before; why should it suddenly depend on it now?

Gene and I realized we had been asking the wrong questions: Why can't we make love anymore? Who or what is to blame? Why can't it be like it was before?

Now we dared to ask some questions new to us. Who says there is only one way to enjoy sex? Who says that one way is the only right way? Who says only soft, smooth, unblemished skin is nice to touch?

If all of us can work our way through the clutter of

advertising copy that covers the desk tops of our minds, we may discover an elemental truth: sex alone may well depend on physical attractiveness, but sex in a loving relationship sees no ugliness of form. The old adage, love is blind, holds a significant truism that graces not only the lives of the disfigured, disabled, and deformed, but of every person who struggles under the impossible image of physical perfection laid upon us. The person who discovers that essential truth before time begins to work its tricks carries a gift into old age.

I had had a fleeting glimpse of that truth years before the fire. It was at the same time I discovered the meaning of "The Velveteen Rabbit," and had typed and framed the passage in the hope that I would not lose the insight. I had accidentally happened upon a scene in my parents' home. Coming down the hall, I had glanced into their bedroom through the half-opened door. My father was lying on the bed, a shell of the robust handsome man he had once been. Several strokes had left him with little control over his own body. He could no longer manage even his most personal needs himself, but depended upon my mother.

As I had visited in their home that summer, I was filled with sadness over the ugliness of his sickened body. Yet as I looked briefly into that room, I saw my mother sitting at the foot of his bed, gently holding his wrinkled foot in her hand, clipping his toenails. The tender acceptance and love in her face told me that she saw nothing ugly about that dear old man. For over fifty years she had loved him, and to her he had become REAL. And as the skin horse said, "Once you are REAL you can't be ugly, except to people who don't understand."[4]

Once I had held that understanding in my hands. My son Jack had reminded me of it when I had first begun my journey through fire. Was it possible, was it probable, that I had become REAL to Gene?

Slowly we began to grapple with those ambiguous, invisible writers of advertising copy and push them right out the door of our lives. We forgot about how it was and concentrated on how it could be. Sex is redefined for all of us through the different stages of our lives, usually unconsciously. Gene and I simply actively sought a new definition as we searched for new ways to explore our sexuality. We read together *Sexual Awareness: A Practical Approach,*[5] giggling like two teenagers hiding a copy of a confession magazine inside a Batman comic book. "If our kids are old enough to display a copy on their bookrack, we are surely mature enough to handle it," we joked.

Our ever-growing intimacy began to open other doors to sharing our thoughts and feelings about our ordinary, everyday experiences. Like the kind of touching that came one warm day when we were back at home.

It was so warm, one might have thought it was a late September morning, except for the golden tones of the falling leaves. The sky was that shade of blue that seems to come only in October after the nights have grown colder. From five-year-old Alan to retired Doctor White, one by one the neighbors roused themselves from a lazy Saturday breakfast and, with rakes in hand, groomed their yards.

It was a day for neighbors to stop and chat about converting from oil to gas heat, and the prayer breakfast just attended. A day to ride unicycles and for puppies to run up and down along the fence to the sound of rustling leaves. It was a day to be tasted and savored. A day made delicious by the awareness that the loneliness of winter would surely follow.

Gene went outside to join the rakers. I picked up the breakfast dishes, loaded them into the dishwasher, made the bed, put away yesterday's newspaper, and did the other puttering necessary to put the house in order for another day. I did my exercises slowly, enjoying the leisurely pace. After I rode my bike, I went out into the autumn day with Muffie. I went about performing the task my kids always moaned and groaned over. "Is old ancient Chinese proverb," I used to tease them. "Those who own dog, must take up the shovel and scoop."

Glancing over the fence, I saw Gene standing near a pile of smoking burning leaves. An old familiar shiver ran up my spine, and I swallowed hard. It had bothered me when some neighbors first began the task of burning. I had stopped myself from running across the street and cautioning, "Be careful. Please, be careful." Instead, I had drawn the drapes or busied myself in the back part of the house.

Ever since the fire, I have had nightmares. Not about the fire I was in . . . not about me being burned. But, always . . . always about someone I loved being trapped in a fire. It horrified me to think about any of them being burned. Even in the kitchen, I was constantly saying, "Step back from the oven. . . . Be careful, it's hot. . . . Look out, don't burn yourself. . . . Easy. . . . Be careful. . . . Please, be careful." When Vicki showed me a small place on her hand that she had burned one day, I almost cried. I simply couldn't bear to think of the pain.

Now I found myself walking down the driveway toward Gene and that burning leaf pile. "I thought you would bag them," I said. For a few minutes I couldn't take my eyes off the flames and the crackling seemed thunderous. I wanted Gene away from there. I wanted to get a hose and douse the tongues jumping around over the leaves. I knew Gene wouldn't be governed by my fears. There was no way to tell him. No way to tell any of them about the fires of hell. It was a place you had to walk through to know.

While I stood mesmerized, smelling smoke in my nose, feeling it in my lungs, Gene responded, "I thought I'd just burn the ones in front. I plan to bag when I rake the backyard."

Suddenly realizing I was on fire inside again, I turned and went back into the house. There was no use to try to explain to him. He couldn't feel the heat.

Much later, I called to him that lunch was ready when he was at a good stopping place. He came into the kitchen, his face flushed from the heat of the fire. He began to eat his sandwich and then quietly said, "It is so hot. The heat . . . it's so hot. . . . I can't stand it on my face. I have to keep backing away. It gives me some small idea of what you must have gone through in that room."

I kept my head bent over my plate. I didn't want him to see the tears that had flooded my eyes. Being burned is lonely. People try to understand. Some try to enter the world of pain with you. But they can't . . . not even by the wildest stretches of imagination. The nurses and doctors who tend to burn victims admit they cannot possibly know what a patient is going through, and some said, "If I am ever in a fire, I hope I don't come out. I know I couldn't go through it."

Gene reached across the table to touch my hand. "Babe!" That was all . . . but it meant so much. In a very small way, someone I loved had at last gone into that room with me and a little piece of the loneliness was eaten up.

How I ached for our life together to be all that it once had been. I had believed that was impossible. But we had made some good steps in that direction, and didn't times like this morning indicate that we did have some chance of rebuilding after the fire? I had never stopped wanting to be Gene's wife—not once since I was fourteen and we had taken that long walk home together after the Youth for Christ meeting.

I once saw these words written on a banner: We Already Know How to Be Good. Why Aren't We Living As Good As We Know How? The maxim now paraphrased became: You Already Know How to Be a Good Wife. Why Aren't You Being As Good a Wife As You Know How?"

Why? Because I was too occupied being a "good" burn victim. I knew if I wanted to salvage my marriage I had to leave that role behind me as quickly as my progress in healing allowed me to. There was nothing I could do to alter whatever thought patterns Gene had established about the importance of physical beauty. There was no way I could erase cultural barriers raised by my appearance. The only person I could change was myself, the only attitudes I could adjust were mine, the only barriers I could remove were my own.

I had to look inside myself to answer the seemingly ridiculous question Jesus once asked a crippled man, "Do you want to be healed?"[6] Did I really want to give up my excuse for not getting my life back together? Did I want to give up the control over others the accident had given me? Was I ready to leave behind the sympathy and the special attention my disfigurement had brought to me? Being healed meant giving up the security of having other persons assume responsibility for my life. Did I want to be healed enough to pick up my bed and walk?

I knew I wanted my marriage to work. I knew that the major responsibility for its working depended on how far behind me I could leave the concept of self that was based on my body image. So, I went to work on me. Parts of my ego were salvageable. Parts needed a great deal of time and attention to rebuild. My interior needed to be remodeled. If you were to walk into the offices of the Edna Martin Christian Center today, you would see no evidence of the fire that once destroyed it. An excellent renovation has been done. But it takes a long time to discard deeply ingrained prejudices; it is not quickly or easily accomplished. Someday I hope my recreation is as complete as the center's building.

I began to list my assets. My appearance had certainly been one, but it was destroyed. There were others that the fire had not touched, or only scorched slightly. I had a great sense of humor. I was sensitive, caring, understanding, forgiving, creative, thoughtful, imaginative, and loving. I was a neat person and fun to be with.

If that sounds arrogant, remember, please, I see myself as God's creation. Whatever attributes I have are gifts from his hand. It does us all good to list our strengths from time to time. Ask a group to list everything wrong with themselves, and they will complete the task in record time. Ask the same group to list their good gifts, and invariably they sit and chew off the ends of their pencils. I needed to affirm again that to diminish myself, was, in effect, to diminish my Creator.

As I began to build up myself, I became more pleasant to be with. Nobody enjoys the company of a self-deprecating person for long. I heard my husband say, "I was so anxious to get home to you." What a relief it must have been for him to open the kitchen door and find not a weepy lump in the den chair, but to hear a "Hi, honey."

You see, the fringe benefit of my own change was the freeing up of Gene. He could concentrate on adapting his own inner feelings when he wasn't constantly engaged in trying to hold me up.

Mary Jans, wife of the burn victim David Jans, was an invaluable help to me at this point. I needed some extra buoying up and turned to David and Mary for it. Sitting in their pleasant living room one evening sharing cheese, crackers, and cider, Mary told me what a hard time David had believing that she loved him after he was burned so badly. He needed constant affirmation and sometimes she simply ran out. She became very tired and angry because he wouldn't accept what she was offering.

Listening to her, I looked at Gene and we both laughed nervously. I finally heard what Gene had been trying so hard to say. I knew I had to accept the love Gene was offering me. But before I could do that I had to believe I was still lovable. I had to believe he could still find me attractive. And I had to stop trying to make him prove I was.

No small order, that! I knew the only way for me was to act in faith and trust, believing what I didn't believe. I think Peter must have felt something like I did now when he wanted so much to believe. The only way he would ever really know was if he risked getting out of the boat.[7] I began to tentatively test the water with one toe as soon as we left Mary's and David's home.

For months, my response to Gene's affirmation of his love for me had been a quick, sharp rebuff. Each time he had tried to touch inside me with the words, "I love you, Mary," I had angrily retorted, "Don't say that. It just isn't true and I don't want to hear it."

Given that kind of rejection, it is no wonder the words had come less and less frequently. And their scarcity had reinforced what I already believed: it was impossible for Gene to really love me.

But, that same evening as we drove home from the Janses', discussing what Mary had told us, Gene tried again. "I really do love you, Mary. I really do."

"I don't know how I can believe what isn't true," I argued.

"You don't know what is true for me," Gene said. "You only assume you know. If you want to know how I feel about something, you need to check it out with me."

"Do you really love me? I'm so ugly."

"I really love you."

"If that's true, it's incredible—incredibly wonderful."

"It's true, babe," Gene affirmed again, turning to glance briefly into my eyes as he drove.

"Tell me again."

"I love you," he laughed.

I let his words wash over me in waves, accepting them without allowing myself any discounting remarks or thoughts. As each wave receded, it carried away some more of the debris littering my beach.

With my opinion of myself slowly growing better, I was able to accept more and more of Gene's love offerings. At last I could respond to his "I love you" with "I know you do." He could reach out with embraces and kisses and tenderness because his own fear of rejection was eased. And, of course, the natural result of increased physical touching was bound to reawaken other deeper, quiescent feelings. We journey on toward more complete wholeness in our relationship. There are still unanswered questions, gray days, and frustration, but for any couple to feel they have arrived at their destination in their marriage is a tragic mistake they may soon regret.

Certainly progress was when I could sing to Gene, "Do you love me because I'm beautiful, or am I beautiful because you love me?"

There is still a tendency on my part to blame my appearance for every downward swing of desire, rather than to attribute it to normal mood fluctuation, job pressures, real physical tiredness, or, at this point in our lives, middle age. I still may walk into a room of attractive women and feel threatened and "klutzy." Observing Gene relate to "normal" women may still spark feelings of insecurity. Being aware of these danger signs will not make the journey less hazardous, but it can cause us to walk with caution.

Clearing some of the debris out of the channels of communication has helped us on our way. Gene has accepted my word that my anger and frustrations are not directed at him. This has allowed me to express those feelings without foisting guilt on him. When I feel threatened and insecure, he still says, "I'm sorry," but now he means he is sorry I have to tote such heavy feelings around, not that he is apologizing or assuming he is guilty of having done something to cause it.

We are in the process of changing some of the language we use to relate to one another. Gene has given up saying things like, "Hi, gorgeous! You look pretty. Hey, beautiful!" And he remembers most of the time not to wolf whistle at me. I find those things offensive and feel mocked by them, though I know he would never do that to me. These are ways of speaking and acting that had become part of our relationship, familiar and comfortable, and it was difficult for him to break the pattern. But, he tried to understand when I explained, "You used to whistle when you came in and caught me undressed, and I'd giggle and tease that you had planned your timing. It was fun. Now it makes my stomach turn over." With great sensitivity and without being told, he sensed the words I needed and now says instead, "I love you, babe."

In turn, I am learning to stop referring to myself as a deviant, a term Gene finds disgusting, or naming myself ugly, gross, weird, and monster. My constant use of these tags made him feel defensive. They demanded a response from him, and there was none except to constantly repeat, "I don't see you that way."

We have substituted a silly game to take the place of old ones. It's called "Neat and Nice." One week, I am "neat" and he is "nice," until Sunday when we switch and I become "nice" and Gene is "neat." Silly? Of course, but it works. The connotation is that we love, admire, respect the person each of us is. We are nice persons, neat persons, apart from any body significance.

This is a difficult thing for me to admit, because I don't want to think that any possible good came about as a result of the fire, but the love Gene and I have always had for each other is richer, deeper, fuller because of the experiences we have shared. We have spilled out our guts on the floor in front of each other and know each other more completely than ever before. We share an increased respect and appreciation for each other. I have witnessed an unbelievable strength and givingness in Gene. And in turn, I have heard him say to me, "I am so proud of you. You are some person!" We come to each other with a greater sensitivity, a deeper caring, and more at-one-ment and peace with each other than either of us ever imagined possible.

Our marriage was cast into a fire, and its dross was consumed and its gold refined. Or as I said to our good friends Dorothy and Elmer Thomas, "Gene and I have walked through hell together and come out holding hands."

In a very private and personal way, I am beautiful because he loves me.

17

Pick a Color . . .
Any Color

I had already accepted my anger as a useful tool for prodding and pushing me. Now I began to see that my times of despair and depression were not all bad either. Some feelings I had previously classified as "negative" and "unworthy of a Christian," I am holding in my hand, waiting for enough time to pass to properly categorize them again.

During the long periods of depression when I withdrew inside myself, I just sat and thought thoughts. I allowed them to run roughshod through my mind. Some of the voices I heard hurt as they beat me down, voices declaring that my worthiness depended on my physical appearance. One day as I sat there steeped in my own tears, I thought, *I have spent almost all my life feeling devalued. For a brief period of time I knew what it was to feel good about myself, to feel OK, and then, just when I thought I had my parade ready to march, it began to pour.*

Something went *click* inside me and I rewound the tape of my mind and played that one over. What I heard myself saying was this: "None of these feelings are new. I have felt extremely worthless before. I have felt very ugly before. I have felt unworthy of Gene before and was certain he couldn't love me."

There were no loud sirens . . . no drum rolls . . . no fireworks. But this small dawning brought with it a glimpse of light and even the hope of a new day.

Recognizing that I had experienced at other times all the feelings now tearing me apart began to soften the impact the fire had had on my life. I had been dealt a knockdown blow, to be sure, but I had been lying on the mat helpless, as though I was unable to get up on my feet and start punching back. I had without question accepted the fact that I was different, my life was different, and nothing in my world would ever be the same again. Then I began to see that I had been on the mat before. I had sometimes lain there almost taking the full count while I cleared my head and assessed my injuries. But then I had somehow managed to stumble back onto my feet. When I did, I realized I still had resources of strength to draw on I hadn't believed were there.

To carry this analogy a bit further, one might also say that my fans had filled the arena and were cheering me on, sending me the will and energy to get up. I found God in my corner waiting to hold me up awhile, to carefully cleanse the hurt places, and to assure me I still had some of the good punches left that he had taught me.

The single most important thing I had to remember now was that *I* had to get up off the mat . . . by *myself*. My family, my friends, all the people who loved me and cared about me, the doctors, nurses and therapists, and even God, had done all they could to help me. Now it was up to me. I could lie there on the mat, broken and defeated, and just give up, or I could draw on all the remaining strength I had and stand up.

Gradually, I began to digest the fact that my response to the fire was crucial. People had been spoon-feeding me this for some time. Jane had said it when she tried to tell me, "Mary Ellen, you are never going to be the same again. You need to accept that." Dr. Swartz had, in response to my question, "When you are all done with whatever surgery you're going to do, will I ever be able to walk into a room full of people and feel OK about myself?" He had turned slowly to face me and said, "Mary Ellen . . . that all depends on you. You will always have scars." And Gene had, when in his desperation to reach me he had shouted, "But you didn't die, you lived. You can become bitter and ugly inside or you can fight back."

My revolution began as a hushed but persistent urging to come out of my corner swinging. It whispered insistently, "You don't have to take this lying down. You can lick it whenever you're ready."

I began to do a lot of thinking about what my response could and should be. I thought about the doctors, nurses, and the therapists who had invested so much in me. "Why," I had asked, "why do they fight so hard to save the lives of burned persons, persons whose bodies will be scarred, deformed, and disfigured forever?" Of course, the ready answer is, they value life. But, that's not enough! There are things worse than death. The only return on their investment was seeing their patients resume active and meaningful lives. I owed them that!

Then there were those who had loved me to life. They were watching, waiting for their prayers to be answered, for their miracle to occur. Some miracle it would be if I lived the rest of my life in a scarred, deformed, disfigured manner. I owed them a miracle. God had set the stage for a miracle play, but I had to accept the part.

Maybe that's what is meant in 1 Corinthians 10:13: "So far you have faced no trial beyond what man can bear. God keeps faith, and he will not allow you to be tested above your powers, but when the test comes he will at the same time provide a way out, by enabling you to sustain it" (NEB).

L. Robert Keck says it another way. God has already given us power; he has already made us able. But, like any gift, we have to receive it, accept it, recognize that it is ours, and use it! In other words, I had already been given response-ability, the ability to choose my response. The way out had already been provided.[1]

Nobody entered my office the day of the fire and installed a window. It was already there, had been for years, a part of the original structure of the building. The way out was already provided. But in those final minutes, when the heat and smoke invaded the room, my response-ability was vital. I had to choose. No one else could do it for me. Stay in that room and die, or open a window and risk everything by jumping to life. Was I able? You bet I was!

That was "heavy" for me. Accepting that premise meant acknowledging that the fire was irrelevant; only my response to the fire was important. It meant saying, "It's up to you, girl, no one else is responsible for the rest of your life but you."

I'm not much of a "pray-er." I just sort of talk to God as I walk along. So as I discussed with God the amazing truths that had just dawned on me, the conversation went much like this.

"Well, God, I guess it's just you and me, huh?"

"Yup."

"And, you're not gonna do it for me, are you?"

"What can I say?"

"I just want to tell you that I don't like what's happened to me. I don't like it one bit. I hate looking like this, and I think I will always hate it. I think I will always mourn what I have lost."

"I understand; I know what it's like to be scarred, you know."

"I know . . . but I forgot. You really do care about what's happened to me. You really do understand, don't you?"

"You've known that all along."

"Yes, I guess I have. But, there is something even more important to me than my scars."

"I know, Mary Ellen."

"You do?"

"Yes, but tell me anyway."

"It's you, God. . . . You're more important to me than those scars, and more than anything else, I want to be your person. I want you to be proud of me."

"I am."

"God . . ."

"Yes . . ."

"I love you."

"I know."

On a Friday, late in the month of October, I gathered up some articles and pamphlets and mimeographed information sheets dealing with the posthospital care of burns. I intended to sort through them, discarding the ones I no longer wanted, and file the rest away. As I looked through them, I began to reread several of the printed sheets. My eyes lighted on two sentences and I read them over and over. I really didn't need to continue looking at the page because the words had already been deposited in my memory bank to be harbored forever in the vault of my mind: "100,000 persons are burned every year. Where are they?" That was all. Two very simple sentences, but they were enough to trigger my own full-scale revolt.

You see, I knew the answer to the question raised. I knew where the other burn victims were. They were sitting, as I was, in dimly lit dens huddled over television sets, venturing out into the privacy of their own backyards, or making a "day out" of going to the clinic and physical therapy appointments. I was stunned by the gross unfairness of this. In my mind, I could see thousands of persons like myself hiding in attics of their own choosing. Vibrant, working, independent persons in the prime of their lives, who had been "burned out."

Our home had become my attic. Surrounded there by all the familiar memorabilia of a happier past, I had begun to feel safe and protected. I had reclaimed this house as my own as I had begun to do my own housekeeping chores, putting things back just the way I liked them and not in a way that suited someone else who had straightened up for me. Gene's and my relationship sat like a treasured artifact in the seclusion of our home. Fashioned and handmade by the two of us, it was being fired in the kiln of our home. I was secure there from all the bad things that might get at me outside of those walls.

I realized that day that my body had not made me a prisoner. I had chosen my own prison—my house. And I had made Gene a virtual prisoner, too. He just had the privilege of work-release time.

I don't know what was the stronger impetus, the new vision of thousands of burn victims hiding in attics; the startling realization that I was hiding, too; or the over-whelming surge of love I felt for Gene as I realized what I had unwittingly done to him. I only know I made a silent commitment to myself. I would go out. No matter how hard it was. No matter how shocked some people might be. No matter if I had to steel myself each time and bluff it out. I would go out. I would not waste the gift of life I had been given.

It struck me that to save life was not enough; the quality of the life saved was equally important. Burn technology has made giant strides since the Vietnam War. Many more seriously burned persons can now expect to live than formerly when there was little or no hope for their survival. But where are they? I had never in my life seen a survivor.

When Gene came home that evening, I was ready. In a somewhat weak and not very convincing voice I quietly said, "I'm going grocery shopping with you."

Those words opened a door that, when I walked through, took me into a foreign world. I had never liked being conspicuous. Walking into a room full of people where I was singled out always sent my inner butterflies on a rampage. Suddenly I had walked out on center stage. I was the "freak," an object for the curious onlooker.

Admittedly, I did look very strange. With a colorful scarf tied over my Jobst mask, I could easily have passed for the local bank robber. I couldn't blame people for noticing. How could they help it? But people are always accountable for rudeness.

As I walked down the aisle in a discount store, I was aware a man was staring intently at me from across the store. He continued to gawk as he approached me and passed by. I moved farther down the aisle, and then turned to look around at the directional signs hanging overhead. The man had turned around, too, and stood in the very center of the aisle, oblivious to the fact he was holding up traffic as he gaped at me.

People have driven past me in their cars, and then stopped, actually backed up, and stopped in front of me to look some more. I stopped my own car once to allow two young boys to cross the intersection where there was no light to help them. They looked into the car to be sure they understood correctly that I was going to let them pass and burst out laughing. One called back as they reached the other side, "Hey, lady, what happened to you, a fight with a Mack truck?"

Then there was the older foursome who walked out of Sears. Gene had parked at the curb near the catalog pick-up door and run in to pick up my order while I was waiting for him in the car. One of the women in the group spotted me as she walked toward our car. She stopped, bent over, and peered directly into the car window. I turned to look her full in the face, thinking she would back off. She did, but only as far as the rear window, where she continued to stare in. Her friend, noticing her odd behavior, bent over to have a look. Having gotten their fill, they crossed the street behind our car and walked into the parking area. Out of the corner of my eye, I saw one of the men turn and start back. *I can't believe this*, I thought. *I really can't believe this*. But it was true. His companions had evidently informed him of what he had missed seeing and, not wanting to be left out, he had returned for a look-see. He pretended to gaze into the store window for a second and then faced the car to see the "freak."

When Gene returned to the car, I dissolved into tears. He reminded me of an experience I had had only a few days earlier when Granny Ton and I had gone to Lafayette Square to do some shopping. Two days before Halloween was not a good time to try my wings there. A grandmother, daughter, and granddaughter walked along in front of us. The grandmother turned, and seeing me said, "Oh, Cindy, look, look." Of course, all three of them turned around to see. I caught up with them just then, and they began to laugh. I knew instantly what they thought, and so I explained, "I know this looks funny, but it's not for fun. I've been burned and this mask is part of the burn treatment."

They were terribly embarrassed and began to apologize. The grandmother spoke just as I did, "I thought . . ."

"I know what you thought . . ."

"Halloween!" we said together. The shopping mall had Santa Claus and the Easter Bunny, why not a monster for Halloween? We laughed together, and it eased a very tight situation.

Gene and I talked about the two experiences on the way home. I realized one incident had ended with good feelings and the other had made me crawl. Gene said, "You should have just rolled down the window and explained."

"I suppose," I replied, "but I just don't think I can handle too much of this."

"I don't *know* . . . but I can imagine how hard it must be. But, babe, you don't have to face them all at once, just one at a time."

And so we began. First, another trip for groceries. Then a movie. Supper at the Carsons' house. One excursion at a time. Sometimes I explained; sometimes I didn't. But each time was a little easier than the time before. And as I commented to Gene, "At least they're looking at the mask, not at me."

I knew I was using the mask to hide behind. The day would come when I would have to face the world without my mask.

That milepost has been passed, too. After almost eleven months of wearing all or parts of my Jobst for as long as twenty-four hours a day, in May of 1981, I took them off for the last time.

Now I am learning how to use special makeup[2] to cover my facial and neck scars. My first attempts were discouraging. The makeup was thick and artificial looking and made me feel untouchable because it rubbed off on everything and everybody. There was no freedom for me in that. I had fought too hard to have good feelings about myself "just as I am" to become a slave again to someone else's idea of what constitutes beauty. Yes, Ann Landers, I am marching to a different drummer, and I hope to do so as long as the band plays.

In a way, I am glad the initial effect of the makeup was so disappointing. It forced me to go out bare, to face the outside world, scars and all. In the process I discovered I had come to terms with my appearance and had recovered a sense of OKness. I didn't have to hide my scars unless I chose to.

Each time I entered a shopping mall or went to church, I would take a deep breath and say to myself: "You are a special person. You are a child of God. Gene loves you." Then I would let out my breath and walk in, to all appearances as calm, cool, and collected as I had always been before the accident.

I have learned to use the makeup to better advantage now. I no longer feel like a mime when I have it on. I feel better about myself wearing it. I do not attract as many curious looks and that makes me feel more at ease. Other people appear to be more comfortable with me when the redness and scars are not as obvious. But I don't need it. There is a freedom in knowing that.

I have returned six times to Wishard for corrective surgery. Some of my burns formed contractures as they healed. My left arm contracted to my side and my fingers grew together, some as far as the middle joint. My arm was released in one surgery as was the eye that had pulled down. (The right eye sufficiently corrected itself in time.) The fingers were released two at a time allowing a slight increase of function after each surgery. As Dr. David Smith, medical director of the burn unit, said, "We aim to maximize what the patient can do, but that doesn't mean we get them back to normal. Adaptions are made that become the 'norm' for the patient."

The norm for me means picking up a glass with two hands, using my mouth to assist my fingers, and being unable to cut with a pair of scissors. But I can do most of my own housework (don't check the corners, please), wash clothes, iron, cook meals, write, and type. I drive my own car and help a little when Gene mows the lawn. There is really nothing I want to do that I can't manage in my own new way. I am even crocheting, and I wasn't outstanding at that before, anyway.

There are still two places I find it very difficult to go: shopping for clothes for myself and to the beauty salon. My sisters, Esther and Betty, have eased the pain of shopping. Together they sewed a new summer wardrobe for me: dresses and blouses with high ruffled necks and long sleeves. To have pretty new clothes, which concealed many of the scars, alleviated the necessity of hunting through women's wear stores and fortified my wavering self-confidence as I took up my former activities.

A compassionate hairdresser in a small shop in Lebanon stayed after hours when all her customers had gone to cut my hair. The first few times I went to Cheryl I was still in pretty bad shape. But if it was unpleasant for her to work on me she never let on.

Then I regained enough courage to march into "Canned Ego," Lazarus Department Store's beauty salon. It was a shattering experience.

The salon area is open to a corridor leading to the public restrooms. One young man, after noticing me in the chair, must have made five or six trips back and forth to the facility. He even left and brought a buddy back with him. I could feel myself shriveling up inside as they stared. I was a long time recovering from that episode.

I know in my head that my feelings about going to the beauty shop are a hangover from the past admonition: Beautiful clothes and beauty salons are for beautiful women. But I can force myself into both situations now and that is a beginning.

There will be more surgeries—some reconstructive, some cosmetic—as I strive for an appearance more acceptable to me. There will always be the discomfort associated with living in a different skin. I still itch, though not so wildly as before. It is particularly bad during temperature fluctuations or when I stand after a long period of sitting or reclining, such as when I stand up in church after the sermon and the "ants go marching one by one." Michelle McBride, who wrote of her experiences in the 1950s fire at Our Lady of the Angels School in Chicago, says she "dances while applying her false eyelashes." because for some reason standing so still causes the extreme itching to begin.[3] For no apparent reason, different parts of my body begin to hurt, and all the burned skin is more sensitive to scrapes and bumps. My knuckles are usually raw where they have been scraped because of their peculiar, bent shape. I still bleed occasionally when I exercise.

Simple social functions may still fill me with anxiety and frustration. I may drop my knife or fork onto my plate with a clatter, or send food sailing onto the floor. Glasses have an uncanny way of slipping out of my grasp. Some cup handles are impossible. My sleeves have a way of dragging their way through my plate as I continue to struggle to handle my new body. To tell myself that these things happen every day to perfectly normal people is no compensation when others turn to stare and notice my handicap, or worse yet, run to my aid.

I cannot shake hands. That may not seem a very big problem until my husband's profession is considered. Imagine standing at the door on a Sunday morning while one, two, or three hundred persons leave a sanctuary—each one with hand extended. I have three options: Sound like a broken record as I repeat two hundred times, "I'm sorry, I can't shake hands." Ignore the warmth and hospitality offered by a warm handclasp, leaving the other person confused and embarrassed with his arm sticking out in thin air. Or, endure the pain as my misshapen fingers are squeezed.

I have tried holding things in both hands, standing with my hands behind my back, and reaching out to touch the person on the arm. In small groups, with persons I know, I simply say, "I can't shake hands anymore, but I am a terrific hugger." The neat hugs have been a good compensation.

Some people have a tendency to be overly solicitous. They lean forward and bend over slightly as they speak in a tone generally reserved for children, the very old, or the sick. They want to button my coat, serve me at the table, and assist me up and down stairs. Perhaps with the passing of time that attitude will diminish. I hope so. I don't want to be forever "the poor lady who was burned so badly." I want to be me.

Yes! I have been badly burned. Yes! I am different. I am different physically, mentally, and emotionally. But different is not bad . . . just different. And I *am* still "me." *I* was not burned. The promise the Lord gave to the Israilites lives for me today:

> "Fear not, for I have redeemed you; I have called you by name, you are mine. When you pass through the waters I will be with you; and through the rivers, they shall not overwhelm you; when you walk through fire you shall not be burned, and the flame shall not consume you."
>
> Isaiah 43:1-2

January 4, 1980, began like so many other days. By noon it was no longer an ordinary day. Yet this is how it happens. On an ordinary day, a day like any other day, tragedy or crisis tears into our lives. Uninvited, unwanted, unexpected, it rips our lives apart. And we are painfully aware that, though the wounds may heal with time, the scars will remain to tell the story.

You cannot identify with my personal tragedy unless you have been badly burned. You have read of my fear, pain, tension, anxiety, anger, frustration, insecurity, ugliness, and loneliness. None of these feelings are my sole possession.

A young couple waits for fifteen years before hearing a doctor say, "Yes, you are going to have a baby." At last the den is turned into a nursery and a crib is purchased. The nine months are filled with shopping for diapers and bottles, with showers and dreams. At last the young woman goes into labor and enters the hospital. The baby is stillborn.

A teenager develops a bad case of acne and is haunted by the derisive name-calling of her peers, names like "pizza face." There are no dates, not even for the big prom; no parts in the school play, and she never makes the team.

A person we have loved very much dies.

A couple who started out with so much love and such high hopes suddenly find themselves living through an affair, separation, or divorce.

The phone rings late at night, and in response to a sleepy "Hello," a middle-aged father hears, "We are holding your son at the county jail. Will you come?"

You may not know what it feels like to be burned, but you do know what it feels like to be afraid, to feel pain, tension, anxiety, anger, frustration, insecurity, ugliness, and loneliness. You have walked through fires of your own.

Maybe this story from Robert Keck's book will help you as it did me:

> A pastor once went to call on one of his
> parishioners who had just been crippled by
> a serious accident. Expecting the person to

be deeply depressed, the pastor consoled,
"An unfortunate accident like that really
colors life." "Yes," replied the parishioner,
"but I intend to choose the color!"[4]

Tragedy and crisis come to all of us and they *do* color
our lives. We do not choose tragedy or crisis; they choose
us. But we can choose our response.

Choosing my response was not an automatic decision.
It was rather a process—a process I was not aware of until
one day, in retrospect, I realized I had chosen my colors.

The process began as I wrestled with God. I make no
apology for this contest. Recently, Gene had occasion to
call in the home of a lady who had heard me tell part of my
struggle to a church group. She mentioned to him that she
had spoken to a pastor about my talk, telling him how I
screamed out my rage at God as I asked him why this had
happened to me. The pastor's response was, "Christians
don't do that."

If that pastor has never wrestled with God, he has never
received the blessing that follows. I needed God's blessing,
the assurance that he was with me. And so I screamed and
pounded on his door until I received his blessing. Just as
Jacob wrestled God in his dream and had the audacity to
say, "I will not let you go until you bless me,"[5] I hung onto
God until I could walk away knowing he had been with me
in the fire.

Jacob walked away from Peniel limping. Some have
called it the limp of blessing because it was a reminder of the
struggle, the communion, and the blessing. Sometimes I
hold my hands up in front of my eyes, looking at their
grotesque shape and the scars that cover them, and I wonder, will I ever look on the scars that mark my body as scars
of blessing? I don't know. Perhaps it's too soon. I do know
they are a constant, visible reminder of something much
bigger than tragedy and pain.

I cannot say I am glad for the fire because of all that I

have learned about God and myself. If I could, I would change into my old body this instant. In each remaining phase of my life I will probably wonder what I might have looked like except for the fire. I have irrevocably lost an important part of my identity, and I grieve that loss.

When I tried to express these feelings to my mother, saying I believed I would always mourn the loss of my body, she said, "Oh, my dear, I hope not. Surely you will get over that."

"Mom," I asked, "are you over the loss of dad?"

I knew my mother would feel his absence forever. She had told me of the number of times she woke in the middle of the night to reach out to the place beside her in the bed they had shared. The cold, empty pillow confronted her with her loss, and her sense of grief was as sharp and painful as it was that morning over ten years ago when she had received the phone call from the hospital telling her, "Hallie died a few minutes ago." You do not forget what has become, in a real sense, a part of you.

I had lived with my body for forty-six years. In the middle of the night, I wake to feel a cold emptiness and I mourn my loss anew. But life goes on. We make choices. We decide how we will live with our losses. Will we live as those without hope? Or, will we live as resurrection people? We each choose our response.

Richard Bach has written: "There is no such thing as a problem without a gift for you in its hands."[7] Learning to accept the gift is sometimes difficult. I was so angry at my problem that I didn't want its gifts. Gradually I came to realize the two were inseparable. Again it was my response that was crucial. I chose to unwrap the gifts.

One of the gifts was the manner in which God kept intersecting my journey. My love for him has grown as I saw how he protected the essence of me from being burned.

I had always thought my faith was weak. It seemed challenged by every ill wind that blew across my life. Now I know it must have been strong. It not only survived every contest, but grew stronger as it was exercised in the struggle.

The time I have spent unwrapping the gift of me has shown me a person I can like—someone I can be comfortable living with. I no longer feel the need to devalue myself, but instead can claim my whole self as good. My weaknesses no longer seem overpowering. I view them as parts of me still unfinished.

I have learned something about myself that is very good to know: I am a survivor. I have met life in a head-on collision and I survived. It is true that I had an enormous amount of loving support, but, in the end, no one else could walk that valley for me. I walked it by myself, and I survived. To discover that I have been created with vast resources of strength is very liberating. Now I can honestly sing, "Because he lives all fear is gone." There may well be something scary in my future, but I no longer fear being afraid.

One of the most difficult gifts for me to accept was the gift of contentedness. It was not my choice to be disfigured. For a time, I did not want the gift of being content with a second choice. But once I opened my arms wide and embraced this gift, I could say, "I am a happy person—who incidentally is somewhat disfigured."

There was one gift that took me by surprise. When I realized it was mine, I could scarcely believe it. How very strange that now, of all times, that gift should be given to me. The gift of security in my relationship with Gene came as a gradual awareness until, one day, I voiced it, surprising even myself. "I love you and am committed to you. But I am only responsible for my half of our relationship. If you should choose to walk away from me or should die, I will be hurt beyond description. But . . . I will survive." My self-worth was no longer dependent on Gene's love.

I am no longer afraid of my future with Gene. For perhaps the first time in my life, I believe I am important to him. And in the finest sense of the words, I believe we deserve each other. Statistically, our marriage may not have a very good chance. But, as Gene likes to say whenever I remind him of that, "If well over half don't make it, that still leaves a percentage that do. We're in that percentage."

I suppose I had always seen our marriage as a 90/10 arrangement, with Gene bringing the 90 and me adding the 10. Because I have come to recognize my own ability to creatively respond to life, I was able to free myself from that underdog idea. There is freedom in knowing that I bring the gift of myself to our marriage, in the same way that Gene brings the gift of himself.

Among the gifts I am still unwrapping are the unique possibilities involved in cocreating something good out of my experience as a burn victim. Already people have looked at me and seen the miracle of intercessory prayer in action. As I have shared my journey with others, my experiences have been signs of hope in the midst of their own tragedies.

The strangest gift of all was something of a paradox. Who would have even imagined that one day I would be promoted from patient to employee of Wishard's Burn Unit? I had really been excited when Mary Jans told me she would become the first coordinator of the unit. I jokingly told her at the time, "There is only one person better for the job than you. That's me. And I'm not ready yet."

Nine months later, when Mary called to tell me David had accepted a new job in Minnesota, I thought only of how I would miss them. But Gene had other ideas. "Did you ask her about the job?" he queried.

That evening I rummaged in that imaginary trunk of mine, examining skills I had packed there. Then I composed a letter to Dr. David Smith, medical director of the burn unit, applying for the job of assistant administrator of the burn unit, or coordinator, as the in-hospital title reads. A lot of bravado was behind those typewritten lines; I wasn't sure I was ready to work again at all, much less to return to the arena where my life had hung in the balance. But, like a child in the game of hide-and-seek, life sometimes has a way of saying, "Here I come, ready or not."

And so I went from patient to employee. My job involves routine duties, like maintaining data on burned patients and taking the 35mm slides that become a part of each patient's shadow file. But the job is also spun from dreams, like developing a follow-up support system for patients and their families, finding funding sources that might one day endow a chair for a microbiologist who would do research into the various types of infections that cause so many burn deaths, and furthering the development of artificial skin to cover wounded areas.

I also represent the burn unit in the community, developing programs for burn care and burn prevention. This lady, who thought she would never be a speaker again or appear in public again, has spoken to over three thousand persons in less than a year!

A small book by Robert Raines, *Creative Broodings,* quotes these words by Herbert Tarr: "Love isn't to be paid back; it can only be passed on." That's what I'm doing in the burn unit, passing on the life, love, and care that has been given to me.

Just at the point when I thought an accident had brought my life's journey to an abrupt halt, when I believed I would be fenced in forever by the limitations of scars and disfigurement, a whole new road has suddenly opened up to me. What a gift! What a serendipity to find myself listening as someone remarks, "What a tragedy that fire was!" and thinking, *Tragedy? Yes . . . I suppose it was.* "But let me tell you what's happening in my life right now—"

Becoming the coordinator of Wishard's burn unit was in a way the last chapter of my story, the appropriate end to my book.

During the last few years I have realized what Paul might have been trying to say when he wrote: "Rejoice always, pray constantly, give thanks in all circumstances" (1 Thess. 5:16-18). I think Paul may have been talking about a way to respond to the gifts that tragedy and crisis bring.

My life will be forever colored by an unfortunate accident. But I intend to choose the color! My cup overflows with joy and thankfulness as I look in my trunk at the many beautiful gifts I have received on my journey through fire. This book is my tribute to all those who have enabled me to choose the color of LIFE.

NOTES

CHAPTER 3

[1] Mary Ellen Ton, *For the Love of My Daughter* (Elgin, Ill.: David C. Cook Publishing Co., 1978).

[2] Jack W. Lundin, *Celebrations for Special Days and Occasions* (New York: Harper & Row Publishers, 1971).

CHAPTER 4

[1] Mark 8:24, Good News Bible.

CHAPTER 5

[1] "Do-Re-Mi," *The Sound of Music*, Rodgers and Hammerstein.

CHAPTER 8

[1] 1 Corinthians 12:24-26 (Author's paraphrase).

[2] Margery Williams, *The Velveteen Rabbit* (New York: Avon, 1975).

[3] Ibid, p. 16.

CHAPTER 10

[1] "Lonesome Valley," white spiritual, collected by Gladys Jameson.

CHAPTER 12

[1] William J. and Gloria Gaither, "Because He Lives" (Alexandria, Ind.: Gaither Music Company, 1971). P.O. Box 300, Alexandria, Indiana 46001.

CHAPTER 13

[1] Jim Conway, *Men in Mid-Life Crisis* (Elgin, Ill.: David C. Cook Publishing Co., 1978).
[2] Graham R. Hodges, "Two Little Grains of Wheat," *Sermons in Stories for Children* (Nashville: Abingdon Press, Publishers, 1959), pp. 45-49.
[3] John Powell, *The Secret of Staying in Love* (Niles, Ill.: Argus Communications, 1974), p. 182.
[4] Bob Dylan, Poster †444 (Niles, Ill.: Argus Communications).
[5] Isaiah 43:18-19, Good News Bible.

CHAPTER 14

[1] Daniel 3:12-30.
[2] Matthew 26:39 (Author's paraphrase).
[3] Matthew 27:46 (Author's paraphrase).
[4] Robert L. Keck, *The Spirit of Synergy* (Nashville: Abingdon Press, 1978).
[5] Ibid., pp. 142-143.
[6] Ibid., p. 126.
[7] Ibid., pp. 128-129.
[8] Ibid., pp. 130-131.
[9] Ecclesiastes 3:1, 4.

CHAPTER 15

[1] JOBST, Box 653, Toledo, Ohio 43694.

[2] *The Official RCAF Fitness Plan* (Ottawa, Canada: Queen's Printer).

[3] Body Shaper (Available from Miles Kimball, Oshkosh, Wisconsin).

[4] Norman R. Bernstein, *Emotional Care of the Facially Burned and Disfigured* (Boston: Little, Brown & Company, 1976).

[5] Ibid., pp. 14-15.

[6] "Loni Anderson," *Ladies' Home Journal,* April 1981.

[7] Ibid.

[8] Philip E. Jenks, "False Gods Who Have Known Me," The Little Scroll, *The American Baptist* 178, No. 8 (September 1980): p. 3.

[9] Bernstein, *Emotional Care,* p. 18.

CHAPTER 16

[1] Bernstein, *Emotional Care,* p. 210.

[2] Josephine Lowman, "Why Grow Old?" *Indianapolis Star,* 2 July 1981.

[3] Ann Landers, *Indianapolis Star,* 2 July 1981.

[4] Williams, *The Velveteen Rabbit.*

[5] Barry W. McCarthy, Mary Ryan, and Fred A. Johnson, *Sexual Awareness: A Practical Approach* (San Franscisco: Boyd and Fraser Publishing Co., 1975).

[6] John 5:6, Good News Bible.

[7] Matthew 14:28-33.

CHAPTER 17

[1] Robert L. Keck, *The Spirit of Synergy,* Chapter 5.

[2] Corrective Concepts, European Crossroads, 2829 W.

Northwest Hwy., Suite 218, Dallas, Texas 75220.
3 Michele McBride, *The Fire That Would Not Die* (Palm Springs, Cal.: ETC Publications, 1979).
4 Robert L. Keck, *The Spirit of Synergy*, pp. 56-57.
5 Genesis 32:24-32.
6 Richard Bach, *Illusions—The Adventures of a Reluctant Messiah* (New York: Delacourt Press, 1977).